PRAISE FOR *AFRICA RISE AND SHINE*

Jim Ovia's entrepreneurial flair demystifies Africa. Africa Rise and Shine *shows his meteoric rise from humble beginnings to building a formidable bank. This is a wonderful African success story.*

SIR RICHARD BRANSON
FOUNDER OF VIRGIN GROUP, INVESTOR AND PHILANTHROPIST

Jim Ovia has been my personal friend and trusted banker over the last twenty-five years. Africa Rise and Shine *lays bare the secrets to Zenith Bank's success from one of Nigeria's most respected businessmen. Jim's inspirational tale of success against all the odds is an important lesson of how adversity can always be surmounted. His principles of doing business can be applied globally as demonstrated by Zenith Bank's London Stock Exchange listing. This book is an essential read for anyone that wants to do business in Africa.*

ALIKO DANGOTE, GCON
FOUNDER AND PRESIDENT, DANGOTE GROUP OF COMPANIES

When the dust settles and the definitive history of contemporary Africa is written, Jim Ovia will be prominently cited as one of the founding fathers of Africa's modern banking system. Africa Rise and Shine *enshrines how Ovia pioneered the creation of one of the continent's most successful banks, and demonstrates how believing in yourself, aiming for excellence, building a team, and listening to your gut—all with an unwavering ethical stance—frame the model for the next generation of great entrepreneurs everywhere. Jim Ovia's story redefines the power of today's self-made man.*

DAVID APPLEFIELD
FINANCIAL TIMES

Jim Ovia speaks from experience about an exciting and important story: the rise of Africa's banking markets. Not only are they growing faster than almost any other region, they are also a hotbed of innovation, especially when it comes to bringing millions of previously unbanked customers into the formal financial system. It's an important tale that deserves the attention of all.

DOMINIC BARTON
GLOBAL MANAGING PARTNER, MCKINSEY & COMPANY

Having personally negotiated with Jim Ovia to create the landmark Prudential Zenith Life Insurance partnership, I have seen his artistry at deal making firsthand. Jim's ability to step back and take a long-term perspective has been a key factor in his business success. His twelve rules for building profitable businesses, whilst critical for African enterprises, could equally be applied globally. How I wish I had read Africa Rise and Shine *prior to sitting down to the negotiation table with him!*

MATT LILLEY
CEO, PRUDENTIAL AFRICA

AFRICA
RISE AND SHINE

AFRICA
RISE AND SHINE

How a Nigerian Entrepreneur from Humble
Beginnings Grew a Business to $16 Billion

JIM OVIA

ForbesBooks

Published by ForbesBooks, Charleston, South Carolina.
Member of Advantage Media Group.

ForbesBooks is a registered trademark, and the ForbesBooks colophon is a trademark of Forbes Media, LLC.

Printed in the United States of America.

10 9 8 7 6 5 4 3 2

ISBN: 978-1-94663-340-8
LCCN: 2018946745

Cover design by George Stevens.
Layout design by Carly Blake.

This publication is designed to provide accurate and authoritative information in regard to the subject matter covered. It is sold with the understanding that the publisher is not engaged in rendering legal, accounting, or other professional services. If legal advice or other expert assistance is required, the services of a competent professional person should be sought.

 Advantage Media Group is proud to be a part of the Tree Neutral® program. Tree Neutral offsets the number of trees consumed in the production and printing of this book by taking proactive steps such as planting trees in direct proportion to the number of trees used to print books. To learn more about Tree Neutral, please visit **www.treeneutral.com.**

Since 1917, the Forbes mission has remained constant. Global Champions of Entrepreneurial Capitalism. ForbesBooks exists to further that aim by bringing the Stories, Passion, and Knowledge of top thought leaders to the forefront. ForbesBooks brings you The Best in Business. To be considered for publication, please visit **www.forbesbooks.com**.

I would like to dedicate this book to my family, particularly my wife and children, who are a continual source of inspiration to me.

I would also like to recognize my brilliant management team and staff at Zenith Bank. I thank them for their tremendous contribution to the phenomenal growth and amazing success of the bank.

TABLE OF CONTENTS

PROLOGUE

It was in June 2013 when, with the day's mail, came a copy of the latest *Forbes Africa* magazine—the one that happened to have my photograph on the cover. I sat down at my desk, putting the rest of the mail aside. As I stared at the magazine, my thoughts turned back to the photo shoot at

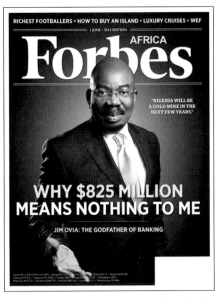

Forbes Africa, June 2013.

which the picture was taken. In the photograph they chose for the cover, I was standing against a dark blue background wearing a dark suit and a sapphire-blue tie. I was looking directly into the lens of the camera, one hand extended as if in greeting. Above, and partly behind my head, was the magazine's iconic name. The cover text read in large letters, "Why $825 Million Means Nothing to Me," and below that,

"Jim Ovia: The Godfather of Banking." For anyone who has sought to make a mark in the business world, a *Forbes Africa* cover is a seminal moment—tangible proof that you have done something not just remarkable, but rare—and for me with my humble upbringing, something quite unexpected.

Though I'm often asked for interviews, I had kept most of the details of my upbringing private until the *Forbes Africa* story. In that moment of seeing the magazine cover for the first time, I realized I wanted to share my story. My cover story gave me a great sense of pride, of course. I experienced a sense of wonder, as well. Many people have asked me over the years how a boy growing up in the small Nigerian town of Agbor had been able to start, build, and maintain a bank that is one of the largest and most profitable businesses in Africa.

The issue of *Forbes* that featured me became the magazine's best-selling edition in Africa. They had to reprint it four times. It was around that time that family, friends, and business acquaintances began suggesting I write a book about my experiences.

This is that book. It took me some time to decide to write it. Certainly, the idea of publishing a memoir or autobiography held no appeal for me; I suspected that, in my case, such an account would do little more than bore its readers. I prefer a book that is less memoir, and more business-focused—a book that describes my business transactions and high-powered deals and details my experience as an entrepreneur. My business ambition is closely entwined with my vision of a future both dependent on and enhanced by various exogenous factors. Like any successful business builder, there are also personal qualities and experiences that prove influential or are carried over into my decision-making process. I want to shed light on the principles and practices that have brought such achievements to me—to provide insight not just for bankers, but for people of all roles and in all industries. It has been my wish for a long time that the young people of my home country of Nigeria—and through-out Africa—take advantage of the tremendous opportunities Africa has to offer. The path to success is accessible to every young African person, regardless of background, family income, or education. This has been said many times, but I repeat it sincerely now—*if I can do it, you can, too.*

AFRICA RISE AND SHINE: FROM HUMBLE BEGINNINGS TO $16 BILLION

Africa now has a fast-growing middle class: according to Standard Bank, around 60m Africans have an income of $3,000 a year, and 100m will in 2015. The rate of foreign investment has soared around tenfold in the past decade.
—*THE ECONOMIST*, "AFRICA RISING," DECEMBER 2011

When most people outside of Africa visualize the continent, the associations they often make are with famine and poverty, conflicts and war. From the moment I began writing this book, I have been determined to redefine this narrative and illustrate the real Africa behind the headlines. The Africa of my birth and of my life experience is a continent of abundant human and natural resources, immense and diverse investment opportunities, and an economy that is primed for leapfrog strategies. Africa's challenges may appear daunting to most, but to those with the right entrepreneurial vision, challenges always provide opportunities. Poor infrastructure? The entrepreneur sees that as a chance to leverage structural improvements as a core component of a burgeoning brand identity. Inadequate supply of electricity? The entrepreneur identifies such a deficiency as a blank slate on which a new electricity supply can be built. My own road to success is evidence that these are no mere platitudes. The path I followed for more than twenty years in building Zenith Bank from a nascent business with $4 million in shareholders' funds to an internationally recognized brand and institution with more than $16 billion in assets was achieved under both military and civilian regimes, despite a decaying infrastructure and periods of economic instability. For anyone who has the intuitive entrepreneurial capacity to envision obstacles as entry points to brand building, and the vision to translate "not yet" into "finally now," the climate in Africa can provide a richly fertile bed in which to seed new business.

In May 2000, *The Economist* magazine published a cover story that dubbed Africa "The Hopeless Continent." Over a decade

The Economist, December 2011.

later, that same magazine categorically reversed its position in a new cover story called "Africa Rising," which was accompanied by an illustration of a young child racing through the grass while flying an Africa-shaped kite painted with all the colors of the rainbow. The story revealed that Africa herself had, in fact, never been hopeless, and it was this awakening perception of a continent at the zenith of her growth that I want to reflect in titling this book *Africa Rise and Shine*.

In the course of Zenith Bank's own journey to "rise and shine," the business began as a single branch in Lagos on the ground floor of an improvised residential duplex that we shared with a private tenant and his wife. At the time, there were no high-rise office structures in the area, and we were not able to afford a stand-alone building of our own, so we created an impromptu commercial space where we could carry out the banking business. We put up our signage and logo, but truly it did not resemble an office or a bank at all. That unassuming duplex was the starting point for a business that became a London Stock Exchange-listed company with operations in the UK, China, UAE, Ghana, Gambia, Sierra Leone, with more than 400 branches and business offices in Nigeria. What lessons can the next generation of entrepreneurs learn from the meteoric rise of Zenith Bank?

Among the most important of those lessons may be my experience that it is not necessary to be born rich or in influential circles to achieve success. By those standards, my own achievements would be categorized as having come about against the greatest of odds. When I was just four years old, my father—who was in his mid-fifties—suffered a massive heart attack and died several weeks later due to inadequate medical facilities. Left to fend for herself and her family, my newly widowed mother called upon her intuitive entrepreneurial skills to set up her own small trading business. My oldest brother, who was almost twenty years my senior and working in Lagos, sent part of his wages home each month to help pay my school expenses. For this reason, I was able to stay in school. This was the emotional inspiration that would ultimately result in my building James Hope College and offering scholarships to 50 percent of its students. My brother's financial generosity and wisdom in knowing how crucial it was that I remain in school are the reasons I place so much importance on education, and on creating programs and scholarships that will help young Nigerians go to school and graduate.

From my earliest recollections, this was the model on which I based my own behavior—and I developed my own work ethic in keeping with my mother's and my brother's example, responding to adversity by cultivating the capacity to react. Throughout my life, I have retained this drive to overcome any and all obstacles life might cast in my way.

The difference in attitude between those two *Economist* cover stories—from Africa-as-hopeless-continent to Africa-as-rising-nations—carries its own valuable lesson: never allow the perceptions of others to play a substantial part in your own vision of yourself and your future. It is imperative to rely on one's own instincts in taking stock of one's own capabilities, and in evaluating a new business opportunity. No matter how fertile the economy, certain universal rules apply regarding properly researching and evaluating potential venues and partners. As I encourage entrepreneurs to seize the opportunity to invest in Africa, I also offer a reminder that the universal rules of prudence apply, just as they do anywhere in the world. An entrepreneur must ensure that due diligence is carried out in setting up any new business, regardless of the location.

It is important to remember that Zenith's level of success is set against this backdrop as Africa rises and shines. In a 2014 article in the World Economic Forum agenda, authors Paul Collier and Acha Leke remark on the fact that the size and worth of Nigeria's economy has been too often overlooked.

"What is lost in most discussions about Nigeria today," they write, "is the strong economic record that it has established over the last decade. In fact, a recent year-long study of the country by the McKinsey Global Institute (MGI) showed that, over the next fifteen years, Nigeria has the potential to become a major global economy."

It remains something of an open secret that Nigeria has become a major player on the global economic stage. I am among a number of Nigerian corporate leaders who are regularly invited—along with heads of state—to participate in multinational summits such as the World Economic Forum, the Bloomberg Global Business Forum, the Commonwealth Business Forum, and the United Nations Global Compact Group. In the elite world of these international summits, it has long been acknowledged that Nigeria is both a major corporate player, and a paradigm for business/private-sector partnerships to accomplish charitable projects. For that reason, another goal in writing this book is to make potential investors and entrepreneurs, both in Nigeria and abroad, aware of the scope of unrealized business opportunity here.

In the chapters that follow, you'll be given an insider's guided tour of the business and branding principles that can accelerate growth in the already fruitful African business climate. From building a brand to developing the art of negotiation, I will present learnable skills and rules that anyone can adopt.

My greatest hope for this book is to demonstrate through example that an entrepreneur is, in essence, a self-made entity who may well be cultivating skills and honing instincts years before identifying them as business inclinations. The very fact that you are reading this book means that if you are not already a successful entrepreneur, you have the instincts to become one. I want to close this chapter by listing some of my own basic business ingredients for success, which are as applicable anywhere in the world as they are in Africa. Even if you are just starting out, I suspect that many of these adages will feel familiar to you—as if you already know them on an intuitive level. Each of these (and more) is expounded upon later in the book, but in short:

FOLLOW YOUR INSTINCTS. If your gut tells you something is right, listen to it. An entrepreneur never takes what he or she is told for granted. (Even *The Economist* gets it wrong sometimes.)

FIND THE ASSET IN ADVERSITY. Any adversity, be it economic or personal, brings change—and change always brings opportunity. It is demonstrable that, whether nations or individuals, those who have the least also have the most to gain, leading to fortitude and an unshakable work ethic.

BRAND MATTERS. Take time from the get-go to think through every aspect of your brand. With enough foresight and strategic planning, a powerful brand concept can be the single deciding factor for the success or otherwise of your business.

IF YOU BUILD IT, THEY WILL COME. Never view a lack of resources or an inadequate infrastructure as an impediment. On the contrary, having the opportunity to instigate infrastructural change is a great boon, with the dual outcome of priming the business pump and ensuring a supportive and happy consumer base.

LOCATION, LOCATION, LOCATION. Start locally, but plan globally. Address the needs of the local consumer first, but make sure your business plan is structured for expansion.

REACTION FACTOR. Good timing is key. Don't let impatience win the day by starting your business too early. Make sure you have strategized in advance, so that when opportunity unexpectedly arises, you are ready to seize it.

INNOVATE, INNOVATE, INNOVATE. If you don't make a friend of technology, it may become your enemy. The trend toward rapid tech development will continue indefinitely. Make the presumption that the tech of tomorrow is accommodated in the plans you make today.

KNOW WHEN TO GO IT ALONE. Growth is not a universal good. There may come a time when mergers and acquisitions will work to your advantage, but more often they will not. Make the preservation of your corporate culture and your shareholder value a priority, and above all else, advocate for your consumer.

NETWORK, NETWORK, NETWORK. Place more value in who you know than in what you have. The entrepreneur sees a potential ally in everyone. Establish your network one person at a time by being reliable and patient. Pave the way instead of burning your bridges.

ALWAYS REMEMBER "CAVEAT EMPTOR." Whether in your own community or in new territory, always use research to carry out proper and professional due diligence, and equally important, remember to Know Your Customer.

PASSION IS EVERYTHING. Cultivate a sense of passion in everything you do, from business to hobbies, and value that trait in others. Entrepreneurial passion is crucial for the success of any enterprise. A business that is conceived to be meaningful and engaging to the entrepreneur is far more likely to succeed than a business designed with the sole goal of making money.

RETURN THE KINDNESS. For an entrepreneur's successes, there are always multiple debts of gratitude to the family, to the community, and to the businesspeople of yesterday who paved the way. There is no higher investment return than that derived from education. Being vested in a sustainable future for your own community is the activity that determines whether a venture is a flash in the pan or a foundation worthy of an empire.

It is about this last adage that I feel the most strongly. The boy I once was—growing up without a father—might never have looked beyond the confines of that small town were it not for one crucial factor: education. I was able to remain in school due to the wisdom of my mother and older brother who recognized its importance and made sacrifices to jointly ensure that my tuition would continue to be paid, year after year. This is the entire impetus behind the creation of the Jim Ovia Foundation—a personal imperative to help support the next generation of entrepreneurs and professionals as I myself was supported, by paying for the tuition of hopeful students in the foundation-created James Hope College, and by providing young people with access to training programs, grants, and scholarships, all to support a thriving African future.

Anything that I have done, you can do too. If you are an entrepreneur with a vision, you can find guidance in these pages and confidence in the Zenith model and ascent. If you are already a professional, seeking to expand your business arena and explore uncharted commercial territory, you will find a wealth of strategic insight in the ensuing chapters. I offer a hearty welcome to anyone ready to benefit from and contribute to a rising, thriving Africa.

BASIC INSTINCT: GOING WITH THE GUT

*I rely far more on gut instinct than researching
huge amounts of statistics.*
—RICHARD BRANSON, FOUNDER OF VIRGIN GROUP

Many people ask me what skill I consider the most crucial to becoming successful in business, or indeed, in any endeavor. My answer often takes people by surprise, but it is very simple: listen to your gut. Everyone has experienced that feeling of an instant reaction or intuition about something that is not based upon data, knowledge, or logic. An investor, for example, hears about a new business opportunity and immediately thinks, *this is a great idea and will turn a nice profit.* Then doubt creeps in. The investor starts second-guessing his initial reaction. *But who knows? I could end up losing my shirt. Forget it.* Everyone has gut instinct, or feelings. The difference is that while some take those feelings very seriously, others are fearful of relying on them, because they are a single interior source. As a result, they don't have the confidence or will to act on that instinct. What determines whether a great idea can ever come to fruition is the initial will to act on instinct—and will is powered by a deep belief in the credibility of what you feel in your gut.

Behavioral economics—the study of psychology as it relates to the decision-making process—defines two systems of decision-making. The first, often called System One, is essentially the gut reaction, a function of intuition. The second—System Two—is the analytic process, a function of conscious deliberation. Humans use one or the other of these two systems when making a decision, and sometimes the choice is obvious. If you see a ball flying at your head, you duck—a System-One gut reaction that is instantaneous. If you are thinking about buying a new car, you consider price, mileage, safety features, and other details—a System-Two reaction of careful deliberation that takes time. In business, an argument can usually be made for either system. Personally, I place a higher value on System One.

My career could be plotted on a graph as a series of gut decisions that propelled me further and further ahead of the pack. Most significant has been my interest from a young age in emerging technologies that simply did not exist in Africa, and basing decisions on the belief that mastering and incorporating them into business—especially computer and internet technology—was imperative for any business wishing to survive and grow in the future.

My interest in computers dates all the way back to my college days in the United States, when I was attending Southern University in Louisiana. After taking several computer-science classes during my sophomore year, I fell in love with the efficient, logical behavior of the IBM machines, at the time larger and more unwieldy than a deluxe television set. I was simply amazed that by punching a card with a few simple commands in COBOL (computer business oriented language) and Fortran (formula translation), the computer would then print out long rolls of all the requested data. I remember thinking, *This is phenomenal! I must learn how this technology works!*

I was quite inclined to make computer science my major, but my college advisor convinced me to focus on business management and administration instead. I enrolled in the appropriate classes, but my passion for computers had fully taken hold of me, and I would sneak into the computer-science room whenever I had the chance. As I gained more and more insight into the inner workings of computers, I began to wonder how this technology could be used and applied in the business world. To put things in perspective, this was 1975. Bill Gates and Paul Allen had just established their new company, Microsoft, after designing the world's first programming language for personal computers. Steve Jobs and Steve

Wozniak had not yet debuted their first Apple computer at the Home Brew Computer Club. Michael Dell was eight years away from graduating high school. 1975 was also the first year that what we then called a "microcomputer"—the ancestor of today's personal computers—was made available for sale to the general consumer. The introduction of the Altair 8800 proved to be the foundational event that launched the personal computer revolution over the next several years. In 1975, the average person's understanding of computer technology was virtually nil.

How, then, can I explain my fascination with these devices, my determination to learn all that I could about them? Why did I feel I must work with computers years before realizing that such knowledge would be crucial in developing my own business in the future? My fascination with and enjoyment of computers gave rise to a deep-seated belief that this technology was the key to the future of all business. Years later, when creating a model for my first major business venture, I knew that incorporating digital technology and internet capability was imperative, even though there was no internet in Nigeria at the time.

Intuition is closely connected with passion, inspiration, desire, and the human aspiration to achieve something unusual, to follow a path that leads away from the accepted norm. Bill Gates did not sit up all night writing code because he knew it would bring him unimagined levels of fame and fortune. He did it because he loved it, and because his intuition told him he was onto something big.

In my senior year at university, I got a night job as a computer operator at the Baton Rouge Bank and Trust. It was a greatly fortuitous circumstance for me. I was now being paid to acquire the training I so craved. Each night, I would type in every transaction that had occurred at the bank that day. Once completed, I created a transaction printout for the bank manager. It was not a particularly complicated job for me, but I count it among my most remarkable experiences because of the level of insight it gave me into how an American bank was using data processing technology to its advantage.

My university years were the foundation of all that was to come. After receiving my bachelor of science in business administration in 1977, and getting my MBA from the University of Louisiana in Monroe in 1979, I returned to Nigeria to begin my service year for the National Youth Service Corps (NYSC) program. We have no mandatory military service in Nigeria, but university graduates are required to devote twelve months to NYSC work. The purpose of this program is to foster both a work ethic and a sense of national loyalty in the hope that young people with good education and bright minds will decide to use those qualities to benefit Nigeria.

My NYSC activities happened to be scheduled in such a way that I was free each day after 3 p.m. I decided to fill that free time with a second job, writing feasibility reports for manufacturing companies—a skill I learned during my MBA program. I made far more money doing this work than from my NYSC job, and by the end of the year, I had not only amassed a reasonable amount of savings, I had also honed my business-writing skills while simultaneously learning about the inner workings of Nigerian businesses. The skills I developed were important assets that would give me a head start when I was ready to make my next career step.

In the last quarter of 1980, immediately after my NYSC program, I joined International Merchant Bank (IMB), a subsidiary of First National Bank of Chicago as a financial analyst. My salary was ₦7,500 naira per annum which was equivalent to $8,800 (at the exchange rate of ₦1 to $1.18). This amount was, at that time, considered to be a very good pay because the price of a Peugeot 504 car, a popular car for the middle class, was about ₦6,000.

At IMB, I received excellent training from very experienced bankers, some of whom gained their education from Ivy League schools in the United States, Russell Group Universities in the United Kingdom, and first-class universities in Nigeria.

The experience I gained at IMB was in the areas of financial analysis in the credit department, treasury management, developmental finance, and trade finance. All of these experiences prepared me for bigger things to come.

Like many other Nigerians, I was intrigued with the opportunities that obtaining a banking license could provide. Following the collapse in oil prices in the early 1980s, Nigeria implemented a Structural Adjustment Program (SAP) in 1986. The goal of the SAP was to restore health to Nigeria's economy, in part by extending opportunities to the private sector through commercializing or privatizing previously regulated industries. In the banking industry, the liberalization of the financial markets meant opportunities for private investors to be licensed to operate banks. When I learned of this opportunity, I decided to make an application to acquire a banking license. There were two types of banking licenses issued in Nigeria at that time—those for merchant banks and those for commercial banks. The latter required a higher equity contribution of ₦20 million ($4 million) from investors and entailed more difficult business operations, therefore many chose the easier route of applying for a merchant-bank license (equity contribution of ₦6 million [$1.2 million]). My gut told me to go the more expensive, complicated route—the road less travelled—so I decided to apply for a commercial banking license instead.

I had no hard evidence to indicate that I was likely to be one of the fortunate few to be granted one of these banking licenses by the Central Bank of Nigeria. By all accounts, there were already a thousand other entrepreneurs on the waiting list—some for as long as three years. By all appearances there was nothing special about me, nothing that might give me a clear edge over all the other entrepreneurs. My thought process at the time was governed by basic instinct. I had a strong sense that if I wrote my own application (rather than hiring someone else to do it), and took the time to create a thorough and compelling business plan, I would be granted the approval of a banking license.

And with that conviction, I *did* have something that gave me an edge over my competition—self-confidence. My belief in my own instincts was one of my most important assets. In fact, research bears out that many successful executives share this belief. In a global survey of 154 top executives, *The Economist's* Intelligence Unit found that 73 percent of respondents placed trust in their own intuition, and 57 percent said that if data contradicted their gut feeling, they would have that data reanalyzed. One of the survey participants was quoted as saying, "You need to live in intuition and gut feeling: mechanized decision-making squeezes out entrepreneurial spirit."

I could not agree more. When instinct is successfully followed, confidence and self-esteem grow exponentially. The effect is as dramatic as a booster on an Apollo rocket. The rocket can get itself beyond the earth's atmosphere, but to travel any farther, it needs the booster to send it places once thought impossible to reach. Confidence and self-esteem—they act as that booster. That may sound too simplistic—especially in its implication that it is possible for anyone to accomplish great things—but simplicity *is* my intention. It is particularly important to me to communicate to Nigeria's youth that if they focus and commit to their work, and if they trust both themselves and the environment of their upbringing, then the sky is the limit, regardless of who they are. What better proof is there—how else is it possible that a boy born into a poor family in a small Nigerian village was one of the first to adopt the internet in Nigeria and founded one of the most profitable banks on the continent? I am that proof.

THE POWER OF NEGOTIATION: INSTINCT AND TRUST

For me, relationship is very important. I can lose money, but I cannot lose a relationship. The test is, at the end of a conversation or a negotiation, both must smile.
—SUNIL MITTAL, FOUNDER AND CHAIRMAN OF BHARTI ENTERPRISES

D uring the period of my national youth service in Lagos, I drove an old beat-up car that my uncle had given to me. Between the age of the vehicle and the wear and tear brought on it by frequent use, potholes, and the notorious traffic congestion, I needed to have the body repaired several times. I found a good mechanic who was able to make the necessary repairs, but he did not have the original paint color, so my car was a patchwork of various colors and shades. Nonetheless, I was pleased with his work, and during the time he was repairing my car, I made friends with him. When at last my car was ready, I asked the mechanic, "Tell me something, would you also be willing to fix other cars for me?" Now that I owned my own vehicle, I had noticed how many other people in Lagos were driving around old autos with signs advertising them for sale. There certainly seemed to be an excellent supply of beat-up cars around, if someone happened to know a trusted mechanic.

"Would these be your cars?" the mechanic asked.

"Yes," I told him. "I'm looking to buy old cars and have you fix them for me. Are you interested?"

This seemed like an acceptable partnership of sorts, so the mechanic agreed. This is how I found myself in the part-time business of buying old cars and having them towed to the mechanic's workshop. This might seem a reckless way to part with my money, but remember, I had just completed my MBA degree, and was always looking for opportunities to apply the skills I had acquired. The cars that I had restored would have to be sold, and I had a feeling, not just that there was a demand for them, but that I would have a knack for this kind of sales.

In his 2013 bestseller *To Sell is Human*, Daniel H. Pink explored the negative concepts that people have of the sales aspect of business. Many of those interviewed, Pink found, described used-car salesmen with adjectives such as "pushy," "manipulative," and "dishonest." What Pink found in his decades of research on work management and behavioral science is that a truly successful businessperson, even a used-car salesman, will have a deep-seated belief and conviction that what he or she is selling is a good thing. This strong belief in the product proves to be a significant factor in how successful a salesman can be, and will work against the slick, double-talking stereotype so many consumers ascribe to those in sales.

As my mechanic began to finish one job after another, I had in effect started a used-car business, one automobile at a time. The mechanic would fix each one up for me—repairing dings and replacing headlights, windshield, bumpers, tires—everything to make the cars look fairly presentable again. On completion of the repairs, I would display a prominent for-sale sign on the vehicle and drive it around, fishing for buyers. Due to the costs of licensing and paying the mechanic for both his labor and the parts, I had to mark up the price considerably from my own purchase price—but, nonetheless, I always made sure it remained low enough to attract a buyer. Once a buyer expressed interest, the deal was always the same—you give me cash, I give you a self-made receipt, and you drive it away right now.

I sold most of these refurbished cars for double, and even triple, the price I had paid for them. The extra income was of great help, but what was invaluable about the experience was that it gave me an arena to develop my power of negotiation.

The used car business helped me discover that I had a natural ability for negotiation. Whenever I negotiated, whether with the original car owner, the mechanic, or the buyer, I seemed to have recognized the principle of win-win situations. Negotiation cannot be learned from a script—it is different every time. The quality of authentic belief in what you are selling (or buying) in a negotiation is very important, but in and of itself is not enough. You must also make the other party understand that you are actively listening and considering his or her own welfare. The course of a good negotiation, whether it is for a single car or the sale of a business, should always be fluid and adaptive. Showing respect and understanding of the person with whom you are negotiating creates an underlying sense of trust—and trust is the rocket fuel of negotiation.

Above all, one must remember that the driving force of sales is neither money nor personal feeling. As Harvard Business School professor Deepak Malhotra has said, "At the end of the day, negotiation is always fundamentally about human interaction." This is very true. Whether it is a young person selling a used car in Lagos, or an experienced CEO making a corporate deal, a business transaction is, at its core, a *human* transaction, and the ability to interact and engage with another person is the foundation of all strategic relationships. To all this prevailing wisdom, I would add something that has always served me very well—the buyer of this moment may be the seller of next year—today's mechanic may be tomorrow's manufacturer. I have always taken every opportunity to create relationships along the way, and it is always an asset in the future. Build bridges in negotiation, don't burn them!

I continued selling old fixed-up cars for as long as it was a profitable way to use my idle time. As my year of national youth service came to an end, I applied for and received a job at the First National Bank of Chicago's local subsidiary, IMB. At that time, the FNBC managed and had majority ownership of IMB. My job was to crunch financial statements of both multinationals and indigenous companies, in manufacturing, services, and trading industries. I was very pleased when I was offered the title of financial analyst. I had no intention of letting my colleagues at the bank see me at a mechanic's shop fixing up old cars or driving the dusty roads looking for buyers. Therefore, it was time for the used-car business and I to part ways. Furthermore, I no longer had the free time to moonlight, as I was arriving at my new job at 6:30 a.m. each day and staying until 6:30 p.m.— during which I enjoyed every minute of the work!

Years later, I tackled the first (and arguably the most important) negotiation in my banking career. It involved the Central Bank of Nigeria—the institution that determined which license applications should be recommended for approval. Prior to this time, the government owned and operated Nigeria's banks, therefore only a small number of people had obtained banking licenses. Now the government was becoming more liberal in this regard, encouraging qualified young people from the private sector who were able to invest to apply for licenses to set up new banks. When the officials from the CBN supervision department invited me for an interview, they told me, "Mr. Ovia, we regret, although we are impressed with your credentials, that we cannot grant our recommendation for you to be the CEO of a bank. In fact, we are surprised that you are applying at all, for you must be aware of our requirement that applicants complete twenty years of banking experience to qualify for such a license. You have had only ten years of banking experience."

"Director Sir! I am aware of the rule," I replied, smiling, "but I am applying to be considered, because, as I will explain to you, those ten years I have worked in the industry prepared me adequately enough to tackle the challenges of a CEO." The examiners looked at each other and nodded their heads in acquiescence of my confidence.

I continued, "My work experience began with the International Merchant Bank, which as you know is the First National Bank of Chicago's subsidiary in Nigeria. Following that, I was with the Merchant Bank of Africa, which of course is the Bank of America's subsidiary in Nigeria." I paused, letting the information sink in, and scrutinizing their faces I could see each expression beginning to change.

"As you know," I continued, "These are banks of international reputation, known for their high quality, for the training they provide their staff, for their corporate discipline, and for the quality of their setup and structure."

I went on making these points to show that the training and experience I had gained at those banks was superior—and that, therefore, the CBN should be willing to waive the additional ten years in my case. Intuitively I was feeling a shift in the room. My unshakable belief in what I was selling—my own expertise—was evident to them. Having gained their trust and respect, I listened to what they wanted and needed, and gave them a simple but compelling argument as to why I was the man who had what they wanted. I was conducting a powerhouse negotiation, and whipping up the officials' emotions in support of young professionals being given opportunity to prove themselves. In the end, the CBN directors issued their approval to the Minister of Finance, recommending that I be granted my application to become the pioneer CEO of the new bank, Zenith.

LOGO AND BRANDING

A brand for a company is like a reputation for a person.
You earn reputation by trying to do hard things well.
—JEFF BEZOS, AMAZON CEO

W hen I was writing the feasibility study of Zenith Bank as part of my license application, I gave a great deal of thought about what name and logo would best befit the institution. Anyone who has studied business knows that these basic elements of branding are extremely important components in any commercial venture. Choosing a company name should be a well-researched and carefully considered part of the most preliminary business plan. There are no hard and fast rules to choosing a business name; it can best be described as psychological, making it important from the outset to consider not only who your customers are, but who they may be in ten years.

In an article on branding, *The Atlantic* interviewed the chief marketing officer of Landor, a world-renowned firm that specializes in naming businesses. Two key aspects of consideration—according to Landor's former chief marketing officer, Hayes Roth—are simplicity, and broad-scale resonance. I felt it was also important to choose a name that was unique. A sampling of existing bank names at that time included National Bank, Oriental Bank, Progress Bank, New Nigeria Bank, North South Bank, Gulf Bank, Peak Merchant Bank, and Credite Bank. As it happened, those banks all suffered catastrophic failure, but of course the reasons for that had nothing to do with their names. Conversely, I have always known that the name of a bank does not determine the possibility of its success. Nonetheless, a business name is its identity, and as such is one of the first forms of communication to the potential consumer.

Under Nigerian law, a bank is not allowed to use any part of the name of an existing bank, so I began with a comprehensive list of what names were off-limits. The banking industry can reach national and even international markets, I knew it was important to look for something that would not be limiting by way of geography, culture, or language. I started researching with those qualifications in mind to find a name that was unique, one that would be memorable to Nigerians, to Africans, and to international markets. I knew it was important for the name to have a wide and lasting appeal. In my research in various thesauruses and dictionaries, the word *zenith* came up in numerous languages—including English, French, Latin and Spanish—all with the same definition of the top, or the pinnacle. When I found this word, it was more than an "aha" moment. My whole being said, *Wow this is it!*

Once I had my bank's name, I turned my attention to designing the Zenith logo. In preparation, I studied many of the best known, most easily recognizable logos in the world—Nike, Exxon, Mobil, Mercedes Benz, McDonalds. I also studied the most successful bank logos, such as Citibank, Chase, and Bank of America. The first thing that struck me was their simplicity. I noticed that even though they cut across many industries—oil and gas, fast food, sportswear, banking and finance—many of the logos nonetheless had three things in common: (1) they were simple—easy to read and understand; (2) they spelled out the name or initials of the company; (3) many featured the color red.

My design for the Zenith logo was the letter Z bisected by a slice of white space—with the top of the letter rendered in dark gray, and the bottom in red. Some of my friends and well-wishers told me I shouldn't use the color red. They felt it was too strong a color, and that people would associate it with blood, or war. "It will scare people," some of them said, bluntly. "Besides, no bank in Nigeria has ever used red." In that last point they were correct—no Nigerian bank at that time had incorporated red into their logo. To me, the suggestion that something had never been done before was not a compelling argument to avoid it.

"Look at the flags of some of the most powerful and prosperous nations in the world," I would point out, when met with this objection. "The US, UK, Russia, France, Germany, China, Japan, and Canada. Why do you suppose they all chose to include red in their flags? It is a color of power. Besides," I would add, "red is also the color of love, and I believe people will fall in love with our logo."

As it happened, several years after we had launched that logo, many of the other banks in Nigeria were taking notice of how people were attracted to our bank, and believing in the positive response to the colors, some began to rebrand their logos with a touch of red. Even two of the oldest and most established banks in Nigeria, that had been using yellow in their logos for more than twenty-five years, later changed their color to red after witnessing the amazing success of the Zenith Bank logo.

Ultimately, both the Zenith name and its logo became iconic and award-winning—widely acknowledged as one of the most recognizable logos in the industry. The name Zenith began to appeal to and inspire many other names. I can recall a day when someone sent me a message to the effect that several members of their family had started to name their newborn babies—both boys and girls—Zenith. I felt very flattered—and truly honored—to have created something people liked so much. In reality, this was a function of those core aspects of successful branding—simplicity, broad-based appeal, and the

combination of something that is simultaneously recognizable and unique.

Another branding strategy I put in place that turned
into a phenomenal success was what came to be called the
Zenith Cube. We designed a three-dimensional cube with
our Z-shaped red and gray logo on each of the four sides. The
cubes were installed atop of the highest point of each of our
branches, so the Z could be seen from any direction. There
was a huge response when we put up those cubes, and people
on the streets would smile and stop to look up at them. Again,
nothing like it had ever been done before.

I took all that time and energy to create the perfect name
and logo for my bank in my license application, because I
knew that a powerful brand identity would increase the likelihood of the Minister of Finance granting me the authoriza-
tion to make Zenith a reality. It was not something I could
leave to refine and perfect later. A company's brand stands
for who its founder is. As such, my brand was almost a form
of negotiation in and of itself—my way to sell myself, my
experience, and my vision to the Central Bank directors and
ultimately to the Minister of Finance. So, it is important to
take time at the very beginning to get your branding right.
It is both your creation and an extension of you. Its name
and its very look and feel must be authentic to the world, as
well as a source of personal pride.

LICENSING ZENITH BANK

Expect the unexpected.
And whenever possible, be the unexpected.
—JACK DORSEY, TWITTER CEO

O f the twenty-five CEO applicants that the Central Bank of Nigeria recommended to the Minister of Finance, only three in addition to myself had just ten years of experience. After that, they imposed a *mandatory* requirement of twenty years of experience, and that rule is still in effect today. If I hadn't negotiated as I did, I would have been forced to wait many more years to make my application.

Five years had passed since the liberalization of the financial markets in 1985. Prior to that time, there were only about ten banks in Nigeria, all of which were owned and operated by the government. With the commercialization of previously regulated industries that followed the collapse of oil prices in the early 1980s, private investors were now trying their hand at starting and managing a financial institution.

At the time I was making my application in 1990, new banks were being licensed at the rate of about twenty per year. As a result, there were already 100 new banks up and running. However, I was undaunted by that number—I saw it as a tremendous motivation to apply all my previously acquired business skills to the compilation of the lengthy application document, which included a detailed feasibility study of my proposed institution. I was further encouraged and inspired that some of my erstwhile professional colleagues who had applied for banking licenses had been approved. I was confident that if I worked hard and met all the application requirements, I would eventually be added to the list of recommended applicants the Finance Minister would receive.

I spent many days and nights writing the Zenith Bank feasibility study, and the time I'd spent moonlighting writing reports for finance and manufacturing companies during my NYSC days proved to be an asset, as I had long since mastered the intricate skill of report-writing. When my feasibility report was ready, I looked for a good printing company that could prepare and print the document in first-rate style on good-quality paper and bind it with a glossy cover. The first gentleman I contacted said he was more than happy to get the job done for me. In what I suppose he intended as a joke, he said he had never prepared a bank document like this, and offered to do it for free if he could have some shares in the company. His remark did not sit well with me and made me question whether he was trustworthy. I chose not to employ him for the job, remembering my gold-standard rule—never do business with someone you both don't know and don't trust.

Though it cost me some time, I searched until I found a printing company I liked and trusted. They did not let me down—printing and binding the required one hundred copies at breakneck speed. I submitted the copies to the Central Bank directors, then spent many months with them in back and forth correspondence. All told, I spent the better part of a year participating in these bureaucratic exchanges, but at last I received the long-awaited letter. The fact of my confidence in my prospects did not detract from the thrill of unfolding the single typed page bearing CBN's official logo of a green eagle atop a shield. The letter itself was brief and to the point: "Congratulations, we are pleased to recommend the approval of your banking license to the Ministry of Finance, who is charged with the responsibility of issuing the ultimate banking license. You should now enlist other prospective shareholders to join you to contribute a total of ₦20 million."

Now I was up against another hurdle, this time a considerable challenge. In the previous year, most of the prospective investors whom I had listed in the prospectus and final feasibility report declined to remit their original commitment.

Only twenty-four prospective investors out of the original fifty showed up to remit what they had pledged. Those who withdrew feared there was too much boardroom quarrelling— and actual fighting—among directors and shareholders of most new banks. In one particular case cited, the chairman of a new bank knocked off two upper teeth of a fellow board member, who was the CEO. Ultimately, I was able to round up the required sum in thirty days despite these fears, putting together a complement of shareholders.

The date of April 22, 1990, is one that will forever be burned into my memory. I had just deposited the ₦20 million of investment money into a special account at Central Bank, which was the final step that would activate my banking license. Just minutes after making the deposit, an announcement came over the radio that a Nigerian military officer by the name of Major Gideon Gwaza Orkar had just led a violent and bloody coup d'état against President Ibrahim Babangida, seizing a radio station, military headquarters, and the presidential residence. Everything came to a halt—every business in the city ceased working. Every interaction with government agencies had to stop. No licenses would be issued.

Luckily for me, on the very day the coup was announced, there was a counter coup—the first coup was defeated by other military officers defending the government. After the radio station in Lagos was regained by loyal troops, there was another announcement from a Lieutenant-General in the Nigerian Army, whose announcement went as follows:

"… Fellow Nigerians, you will all agree with me that the reasons given for this grave misconduct are significantly motivated by greed and self-interest. The soldiers involved decided to constitute themselves into a national security nuisance for no other cause than base avarice. Most of these disloyal elements have been arrested and are already under-going interrogation. The remaining dissidents are advised in their own interest to report to the nearest military location and hand over the arms and ammunition in their possession. Long live the Federal Republic of Nigeria."

At the time, the most senior general of the highest government ruling body—the Armed Forces Ruling Council—made a dramatic speech to the nation, assuring citizens that all was well and that business should return to normal. Subsequently, at its very next meeting, the general approved ten banking licenses. The Zenith Bank license was one of them, and with the flurry of governmental confusion out of the way, we were now on our way as a fully licensed bank.

COMMENCING OPERATIONS AT ZENITH BANK

*To be a CEO is a calling. You should not do it because
it is a job. It is a calling, and you have got to be involved
in it with your head, heart, and hands.*
—INDRA NOOYI, PEPSICO CEO

As soon as we received our banking license and registered it at the government registry, we promptly called each member of the senior staff of my bank, to whom we had sent letters of employment four weeks earlier, and told them to commence work during that month. They were not sure *where* to commence work, for we did not have any proper banking buildings. At that time, there was no suitable office building we could rent. I had been using a temporary one-room office, with my secretary handling all the administrative work for me.

Several weeks earlier I had found a residential four-bedroom duplex on Ajose Adeogun Street, on Lagos' Victoria Island. The building was a duplex—a tenant and his wife occupied one side, and our office space was on the other. It soon proved to be unworkable for a bank to share a duplex with private residents. It was not easy for the residents, either, with the noise of cars coming to the bank, and the heavy foot-traffic of customers coming in and out. With the constant influx of banking clients, the private driveway of the other tenants was often encroached upon or blocked. Though it was not my intention to cause them disruption, it was nonetheless unavoidable. I knew it was only a matter of time before they would move away—and within three months they did.

The first Zenith office.

Although I sincerely regretted causing inconvenience to the tenants, I could not help but be pleased with the prospect of them moving out, since it would allow Zenith Bank to have the remainder of the space to do business. That was our inauspicious beginning, but very soon we would be creating jobs for hundreds, and then thousands of people—and paying huge amounts of taxes to the government in the process.

When the first customer walked through the door, I was so happy. He was a director of a Chinese company, a man I had known for about five years. He picked up the account-opening form and filled it out, and within the next few days all the sales of that company were being deposited in the account we opened for him. I had always maintained an excellent relationship with this man in my previous employment. Because of our mutual history, his company decided to reciprocate by doing business with our new bank. This became a story of how fostering good business relationships can pay off in the future.

There were only five senior bank managers, including me, and considering that we had only one customer, this was a good number to start with. Of course, we hoped to build up our customer base steadily, but we set ground rules and guidelines to the effect that we would not accept just anyone who walked through the door. We would only accept those whom we had gone out to look for, or knew enough about to invite.

I established a guideline of a workday that started at 7 a.m. This meant we all had to arrive before then, as our senior-management meetings were always scheduled first thing in the morning. In fact, I had announced that I would lock the door at 7 a.m. to keep out anyone who was late arriving at the office. The reason I adopted this approach was not simply for the sake of being strict; I had seen lots of laissez-faire operations go under, and I wanted to inspire pride in our operation. My own attitude and putting myself under the gun resulted in those management members being so disciplined and committed that in the first year of our operation not one of them was ever late to a meeting. I was so proud of those pioneer senior managers—they were so dedicated and diligent, sometimes they acted as if their personal futures depended on the survival of the bank.

With operations fully underway, we continued to fine-tune our efficiency, our processes, and our speed of service delivery. We took on new employees as it became necessary, and we realized that they would all have to be trained. Every weekend we organized some form of training program or seminar on the premises for all the staff. We would start each of those sessions with a quotation often erroneously attributed to Mahatma Gandhi, but more likely originating from Studebaker executive Kenneth B. Elliott:

The customer is the most important visitor on our premises. He is not dependent on us we are dependent on him. He is not an interruption to our work; he is the purpose of our work. He is not an outsider to our business; he is part of it. We are not doing him a favor by serving him, but rather he is doing us a favor by giving us the opportunity to serve him.

When we opened those seminars by repeating this quote together, it was as if we were saying a heartfelt prayer.

In keeping with their commitment to discipline, the managers were very quick to mount some form of penalty for any infraction of our rules. On one occasion, a senior manager offered some unauthorized loans to a customer without obtaining the appropriate approval. Within twenty-four hours after the huge debit appeared in the computer system, the senior-management committee moved to take immediate and severe disciplinary action against the guilty party. Their mutual decision was to swiftly withdraw the infracting manager's authority to sign or authorize any document—in effect, stripping him of most of his authority. For the next two years after this disciplinary action was taken, no other senior manager ever committed that offense or anything similar.

It was also our practice from the beginning to devise ways to recognize and reward hard-working and exceptional staff members. I knew that employees who were well-treated and felt valued would pass along that treatment to our clients. As Doug Conant, former president and CEO of the Campbell Soup Company, has said, "To win in the marketplace, you must first win in the workplace." My experience as a CEO is that a little public recognition and appreciation of good employee performance always goes a long way.

In those early years, we would publish the names of employees of the month on the bulletin boards to announce to all staff that these workers were outstanding. A letter was then sent to each one, signed by me, detailing his or her specific achievement. In later years, we created a significantly more elaborate annual award ceremony, but the principle remained the same. Conveying appreciation to employees at all levels is easy to do, costs no money, and serves to motivate and galvanize the work force. It's simple human nature. As Dale Carnegie put it, "People work for money, but go the extra mile for recognition, praise, and rewards."

SEEK OUT NEW WAYS
OF DOING THINGS

When all think alike, then no one is thinking.
—WALTER LIPPMAN, PULITZER PRIZE-WINNING JOURNALIST

When we commenced our banking operation, each of the four largest banks in the country—First Bank, Union Bank, UBA, and AfriBank—already had between 400 and 600 branches. Zenith Bank had only four. This is one of the reasons I sometimes jokingly called each of the big-four banks the "800-pound gorilla."

We realized we needed to branch out to different towns and cities in the country. Nigeria is quite large—covering an area of 923,769 square kilometers, (356,659 square miles), bordering the Atlantic Ocean to the south, Niger and Chad to the north, Cameroon to the east, and Benin to the west. Expanding presented a huge challenge. We drew up a strategic plan for opening as many branches as we could, within a very short space of time.

Nigeria comprises thirty-six states, plus the federal capital territory of Abuja. We decided that each state capital must have a branch; further, that each branch must be installed and open for business within three to six months. We interviewed around twelve different architectural firms, and we sent RFPs to perhaps the same number of contractors. Each contractor was required to know exactly what the requirements were for the Zenith Bank branch.

The process of setting up a Zenith Bank branch involved one of two strategies—either finding the land and putting up a new building that would fit the structure of the bank model, or renting an existing structure and modifying it to fit the same model. I visited all the sites to make sure they were in suitable environments for the Zenith Bank brand, and to see that they met the requirements for the look and feel of one of our branches. To do so, I had to cover thousands of miles, crisscrossing Nigeria many times, traveling sometimes by car and other times by air.

On one trip, I was heading to Sokoto, approximately a two-and-a-half-hour flight from Lagos, where our bank headquarters was located. The aircraft on which I was flying was about forty years old, owned by Harka Airline. Its engines sounded like a palm-kernel grinding machine, and the tires were almost completely worn bald. When we lined up to board this aircraft and I eyeballed its condition, I suddenly felt very disinclined to board. The needs of Zenith were more important than my own, and the visit to Sokoto was imperative, so I made the sign of the cross and got on.

The flight lasted for three hours, as the plane flew much more slowly than it should have. When we finally landed at the Sokoto airport and taxied to a stop, the pilot announced that one of the four tires had gone flat from the impact of landing. This was near enough to a close call that I vowed to myself never to go through such an experience again.

For the first five years after I opened the flagship Zenith Bank, additional branches were operating out of a hodgepodge of buildings, most of them very shabby in appearance. You could not tell one branch of a bank from another. I decided then that, as we implemented our plan to place a branch in every state, it would be far better to design them all to look alike. Of course, the idea of design-uniformity and place-branding had long since caught on in the US and other places, but in Nigeria few businesses were using it. However, the principle behind it is applicable in almost any culture.

In *Who's Afraid of Niketown,* Friedrich von Borries describes physical design and architecture as another way for a brand identity to communicate itself to the customer. He writes, "...architecture is now intended to convey the identity of a brand, is now expected in an experiential realm, to be an element in brand communication." That principle has proved to be a vital form of marketing for almost every kind of business, from McDonalds and food, Ikea and furniture, the

Gap and clothing, to financial institutions such as Citibank and Merrill Lynch. I knew that this form of place-branding would be just as effective in Nigeria, and saw to it that each branch of Zenith Bank looked the same; the doors, the roofs, the design, the interior—everything. Customers knew immediately that it was a Zenith Bank they were looking at. I took this place-branding one step further, by ensuring that every one of our branches was located on an attractive street— wide, well-lit, and in good repair, particularly in Lagos, where many roads were in bad shape.

My decision to brand Zenith Bank in its look and feel was a defining moment, and another instance in which trusting my instinct proved to be extremely beneficial. Implementing this kind of interior and architectural place-branding was a game changer for us. It was another factor that made my name in banking. Five years later, most banks were doing the same thing.

Regardless of the distance from one Zenith Bank to another, our focus on a simple and adaptable logo, and our decision to follow a uniformity model in the look and feel our buildings, created a kind of web of connection and unification between each one of our locations. Customers might travel far from

Above and right: the Zenith head office.

home, but the sight of the Zenith Cube and the iconic red and gray Z in any cityscape gave our customers a sense of security and familiarity. In any business, connection is the most vital linchpin between a business and its clients.

I knew there was one more step to take to facilitate our consumer connection and maximize our corporate capabilities. It would be the biggest and boldest step of all, and one that was unheard of in Nigeria at that time—for the simple reason that it did not yet exist in our country. I knew that the long-term future of Zenith depended upon this non-existent web of connectivity.

That being the case, I knew what I had to do. I had long believed that any business that was going to survive into the future must incorporate web technology into every aspect of its operation. Since there was, as of yet, no internet in Nigeria, I had only one possible course of action: *I would have to bring the internet to Nigeria myself.*

BUILDING THE INFORMATION SUPERHIGHWAY

Innovation distinguishes between a leader and a follower.
—STEVE JOBS, APPLE CO-FOUNDER

When Zenith Bank first opened its doors in 1990, there were no ATMs in Nigeria, no debit or credit cards, no digital networks at all. We knew that to attract a growing pool of customers and to be sustainable in the ensuing years, we had to digitize our business. Most Nigerians had no idea what the internet was. This was a daunting prospect—on the scale of deciding to bring automobiles to a country that does not have them. You cannot simply bring the cars—you must build roads on which they can be driven. You must ensure that there are sufficient gas stations built to supply the vehicles with fuel. You must educate young people in auto-mechanics so that they will open businesses to provide maintenance services. You must develop a training method whereby people can learn how to drive. First and foremost, you must find a way to convince a country that has never had automobiles that it is a technology worth their time to invest in and use. This gives some idea of the scope of the task before me.

I remember very well reading in Bill Gates' book *Business@the Speed of Thought* that any company that did not embrace technology and innovation would not survive into the future. So, while the sheer mass of the work and organization it would take to bring the internet to Nigeria was overwhelming, I was more than prepared to take it on. It was not just the future of my own bank that gave me this conviction—this was an investment in the future of all Nigerians. In countries like America, the internet was already being adapted in multiple arenas, from finance to health care to retail commercial ventures.

As early as the 1970s, the concept of what would become known as the internet was the subject of intense speculation by some. Alvin Toffler's 1970 mega-bestseller, *Future Shock*, gave many projections for the future, not all of which were right. The book made a serious case for taking change seriously, and stressing how categorically technology would change the world. Toffler believed that the faster technology *did* change, the faster it *would* change (which is certainly true of computers). In other words, a fast rate of change will naturally accelerate, and people must prepare for that before they are left behind the learning curve. One of Toffler's central themes was that knowledge and information—and the capacity to exchange knowledge and information efficiently—would be the core of the most powerful societies, supplanting the importance of the labor force. He predicted that personal computers and the internet would become the vehicle for this knowledge exchange, and that nations, societies, or cultures that did not prioritize mastering computer technology would be unable to prosper into the future.

Future Shock sold millions of copies; and though Toffler's ideas about the economy (that the market economy was in decline, and the industrial nations would be replaced by post-industrial nations) were very off-base, his understanding of the rate at which change would accelerate was entirely accurate. Any person who wasn't prepared to keep up with these changes would be paralyzed by what he called "future shock." The key was to pay attention and not be intimidated. AOL founder Steve Case recalled reading Toffler as a college student, saying it "completely transformed the way I thought about the world—and what I imagined for the future."

I understood this very well, which is why I knew that the subject was bigger than Zenith Bank—the future of Nigeria was directly related to the country's economy becoming digitalized. Its success or failure as an African economy would in large part depend on how soon Nigeria could embrace the concept and the reality of the internet as an integral part of society. Thus, the process of bringing the physical technology had to coincide with the process of promoting and facilitating its use by the public. With that goal in mind, I founded an internet service company in 1995. A few years later, I became the first president of the Nigerian Internet Group. We worked in conjunction with several organizations both in Nigeria and abroad, including the Nigerian Communications Commission, the National Data Bank, the Administrative Staff College of Nigeria, the United States Information Service, and the British Council.

At the same time, I was thinking very aggressively about the need to set up a data infrastructure company. That same year, I formed a network and ICT-services company which I named Cyberspace (a name I could not in later years have used, as it became synonymous with the technology). Cyberspace obtained a license from the Nigerian Communication Commission to be known as an internet service provider, one of the very first in the country.

The NCC's license to Cyberspace covered the approval to transmit both data and internet services. The operation for the data network was started in June of 1995, but as of then, there was no backbone infrastructure in Nigeria to transmit data via satellite.

At that time, we were still using NITEL, the national telephone monopoly in Nigeria. We used their normal telephone lines, so the speed was very slow. In a country of about 150 million people, the teledensity was so low that one telephone line served 250 people. If you used the line for data transmission, it carried a speed of only 9.6 kilobytes per second. To download data from the US, you might as well go and get a cup of coffee while it downloaded. We wanted to change all of that with our wireless technology.

I had read in the news that a company in Basingstoke, a small town in England, had a gadget that would transmit data on a 2.4 megahertz spectrum—in other words, it used a channel that could operate via satellite without cost. I traveled to Basingstoke to see this device for myself. Sure enough, the equipment for data transmission—which was of US military origin—was exactly what we needed, so I bought it.

In this era, the military regime was not especially open to or tolerant of certain business transactions, particularly those which they did not understand. I experienced this personally when I set up my first VSAT (very small aperture terminal) satellite. A VSAT is a satellite communications system that uses a dish antenna on the ground to interface with a satellite transponder in the sky. The satellite connects a series of hub stations, which use the satellite to retransmit communications from one user to another.

The dish, about seven meters in diameter, had to be installed on a raised platform approximately three meters above ground level. It would then be positioned to track existing satellites that were already orbiting (in our case they were the American PanAmSat and IntelSat, and the

European EuroSat). I then learned that the South African government (South Africa being more advanced economically and technically) was already providing backbone infrastructure for data transmission as a commercial service to companies within South Africa. I realized I could set up my own satellite dish that would allow us to connect to orbiting satellites owned by South Africa's Telkom, and enjoy their services. This seemed to be an excellent avenue down which to proceed. Unfortunately, the Nigerian military government did not agree. In short, they thought our dish was being used to spy on the country.

Zenith Bank's first VSAT satellite.

We tried to convince them that our technology was intended to communicate data reception for businesses and business activity. I went to the office of a general who was acting as the Minister of Communication at the time. I explained the concept of the internet and the VSAT as simply as I could put it, stressing the technology's potential not just for my bank, but as an enormous benefit for the entire nation. He remained unconvinced. I pleaded with him not to pull down my satellite dish, but he made a call, and a military group was sent to do just that. The satellite was pulled down and its transmissions stopped, along with my opportunity to carry on providing internet services.

DON'T AGONIZE, DIGITIZE!

You shouldn't focus on why you can't do something,
which is what most people do. You should focus on why
perhaps you can, and be one of the exceptions.
—STEVE CASE, AOL CO-FOUNDER AND CEO

Since I had been stopped at that time from utilizing satellite technology, I turned my attention to the existing phone lines in Nigeria. I set up an appointment to meet with the managing director of NITEL. No individual companies were yet allowed to provide telephone services, and the telecommunications industry was essentially subsidized by the government, a government that was weak when it came to providing the necessary and adequate infrastructure. Consequently, NITEL had deployed just 400,000 lines.

When I met with NITEL's director, he received me very well, and listened to my argument as to why internet services would be good for business and data dissemination. He proved to be more suspicious of unknown damaging activities that could potentially be accomplished through the internet. "They will never allow internet service in Nigeria," he told me. Fortunately for us, within several years he was sacked (news that I heard on the radio on my way to work) and another professional was appointed. The new NITEL Director was able to understand the essence of what we were doing, and acknowledged the potential to improve the economy and attract services from more developed countries like the US. At long last, we would be allowed to move forward.

Now that we could install our VSAT dishes on the tops of our buildings, we could use them to link communication and transmit data between all our branches. We were the first to do it, and it was another game changer for Zenith. In 1997, Cyberspace acquired a new spectrum frequency from the NCC. The technology enabled Cyberspace to transmit data within Nigeria wirelessly. Cyberspace wanted to improve its technical competence and efficiency. We approached Sprint Global One—a subsidiary of Sprint Corporation USA—to help us out. They were pleased to sign a contract with Cyberspace for just such a collaboration. Because our company was so small and our operation still in its infancy, Sprint decided to send one of their junior officers, Timothy Lancaster, to help us set up our wireless service. I remember him very well to this day for being a brilliant computer programmer.

With Zenith Bank now digitized, the technology had to be implemented very quickly. I was able to ensure that every

Zenith staff member had a personal computer or a handheld device. All processes of the bank were converted to digital forms and computerized, making it easier to transact with customers, transmit transactions, retrieve data, and make reports to regulators. Word quickly spread that a customer could go into one Zenith branch to make a transaction, such as a deposit, then drive to his local branch and find the new balance already reflected.

Now at last, the way was set not just for Zenith customers, but for all Nigerians to take advantage of the enormous potential of the internet. Again, we knew that the onus to make this a reality was on Zenith. Nigeria was, and still is, a country of tremendous possibility and unlimited opportunities, with a large population of young educated men and women ready to embrace technology. They couldn't do so unless some way was found to connect them as people *with* the technology. We started to offer seminars and workshops to do exactly that, continuing the American CTO (computer technology office) program—the technology-driven awareness program offered by the United States Embassy. We invited people to our bank branches or to larger lecture halls by enticing them with the chance to witness internet services for themselves and experience how freely they could download virtually anything. In this way, the internet sells itself—and those who attended our seminars were amazed to see how it worked, and that they could log into businesses or even universities in America.

I was tremendously excited and encouraged by what I saw when I spoke about computer tools and software at those seminars. The seats would be packed with audiences composed mostly of the younger generations. Sometimes a hall designed for one thousand people would have three thousand people crammed inside. Usually the first question I would ask the audience was how many of them had e-mail addresses. Many would indicate they knew what this was, but very few actually had one. Most people I encountered did not know how to get an e-mail address, had no internet connection at their homes, and did not even have the where-withal to spend enough time and money at cyber-cafes to get themselves started.

I had to start somewhere, and my intuition told me to count on the reluctance of this younger generation to be left behind in the new technological age. I told them that, in future programs I would be offering, it would be a requirement that any person wishing to attend had an e-mail address. Those who did not would not be allowed to participate. Once they did that, I promised I would see to it that they had wireless internet connection and service, not one depending on the painfully slow NITEL landlines. If their parents registered with an ISP service like ours, which was using satellite technology to deploy wireless service, the speed and bandwidth would permit them to do things like conduct research about how to apply to universities outside of Nigeria. I showed them how they could connect to university websites and find out everything they needed to know to apply. Those at school locally could use the technology to access university libraries—putting huge resources at their fingertips.

My tactic proved to be enormously effective. No one attending those early seminars wanted to be closed out of future ones. Having tasted the fruit of technology, they were more than motivated to do what they had to in order to get internet access. After several rounds of these seminars, when I asked my audience how many had e-mail addresses, every one of them did. I never had to make good on my threat to refuse attendance to those without e-mail addresses.

All I had to do was provide the opportunity. The influential power of technology and internet services did the rest— and thousands of young Nigerians were acquiring the means and the knowledge to step into the blossoming internet age.

GROWING ZENITH
AGGRESSIVELY

Help young people. Help small guys. Because small guys will be big. Young people will have the seeds you bury in their minds, and when they grow up, they will change the world.
—JACK MA, ALIBABA FOUNDER AND EXECUTIVE CHAIRMAN

n the 1990s, few, if any, banks had any knowledge of how computers worked, or how to deploy them in banking. That gave me a tremendous edge—enabling my bank to make a quantum leap. Now that we had both the hardware and the banking software, we no longer experienced the kind of operational problems other banks had. As a result, we were soon outstripping them in efficiency and, consequently, in customer numbers. My hunger and determination not to be daunted by the task of bringing the internet to Nigeria resulted in the first digitized bank in the country, and propelled Zenith Bank far ahead of its competition!

In those early years of Zenith's existence, I stressed to my managers that the only way we would succeed was to cultivate a deep hunger to do well. I would say to them, "If we have fire in our belly, we'll achieve the results we want. If not, we will be mediocre at best." I wanted to set a good example myself, so I went the extra mile. I would go home every evening with a report of the day's transactions. Working past midnight, I would go over all the customers' names, so I could call and thank them the next day. You can only do these kinds of things when you are genuinely hungry to succeed. However, it is greatly important not to become unlikable in the process, or to forget about those who have been of help to you, or might one day be in a position to do so.

People can always decide to like you or dislike you, and much depends on your attitude toward them. If you create an aura of positive thinking and cultivate fair and respectful ways of dealing with others, you make a lot of friends. For example, I made it my habit to seek to empower people who worked for me by mentoring them, attending their social gatherings, and empathizing with them in their family matters.

They became my friends, but they also realized I was empowering them when I sent them for training and had them attend various conferences, not just to be better employees but to learn to think like a boss themselves. When they came back, I helped them with speeches and created leadership opportunities for them. They began to see themselves not merely as staff members but as managers of people. They saw me not only as a boss but as a friend and a mentor.

People often wonder about Zenith, *What is so special? What is behind its story of success? What is it about the brand that gets its people living out the ideals of its founding father with such fierce loyalty, commitment, and passion?*

The secret of the bank's winning strategy is no secret at all. Zenith has always been anchored on the high premium it places on its people—from employees and stakeholders to clients. Zenith views its staff as one of its highly prized assets, with its core human values of integrity, professionalism, corporate governance, loyalty, and excellence.

We created a policy that only the top students in their classes could work for us, and we advertised and recruited accordingly. For that reason, we had brilliant accountants, lawyers, economists, and customer-service employees. In the latter case, a professional and polished appearance was important, but first they had to have top grades and be brilliant communicators.

Because of our hiring practices, more and more high achievers wanted to work for Zenith Bank. Our staff had the largest number of chartered accountants of any organization in Nigeria—including the government. The National Association of Accountants held semi-annual conferences, but if our accountants were to attend, it would empty our branches. Therefore, the association created a rule to favor us; they decreed that they would always hold their meetings at Zenith Bank.

The people who worked for me remained loyal and motivated, and they understood that I saw the kind of hunger I myself had as an asset in my employees. Once they realized that I not only wanted—but was willing to help—them all to move up the ladder to become the leaders of tomorrow, they were empowered to blaze the path forward and set leadership positions in their sights.

Some people are afraid to take a leadership role; they don't have the guts and are too afraid to take risks. Those who fail in business often do so because they allow themselves to operate from a place of fear.

To pave the way for success and future leadership roles, the employees of today must apply diligent effort, cultivate the desire to learn what it takes to succeed, must be flexible in their thinking, nourish good relationships with coworkers and customers alike—and they must recognize their own hunger as an important asset that is to be valued and nurtured. This kind of hunger creates an employee who is simultaneously committed to excelling at his or her job, and who has the determination plus an expectation that he or she will one day become a business leader. A great work ethic combined with great expectations will open the doors to every possible pathway to success.

Y2K—THE MILLENNIUM BUG

Today I have signed into law HR 775, the "Y2K Act."
This is extraordinary, time-limited legislation designed to
deal with an exceptional and unique circumstance of
national significance—the Y2K computer problem.
—BILL CLINTON, FORMER US PRESIDENT

Throughout the year 1999, businesses, financial institutions, governments, and people around the world began to worry in earnest about the cyber-phenomena referred to as Y2K (for Year 2000). The basis for all this concern was deceptively simple.

In almost every computer program written between the 1960s and the 1980s, years were represented by a two-digit code. Memory and storage costs during those decades were very high, and computer engineers took every opportunity to save space in their programs, hence a four-digit year became a two-digit year, taking up only half the space. The year 1986, for example, was represented in code as 86. The problem stemmed from what would happen at midnight on December 31, 1999. It was possible that computers would recognize 00 as the year 1900, instead of 2000.

Most computer software and hardware are reliant on dates, one of the variables that dictate how the system on that computer will operate. The banking and finance industry, for example, uses systems that rely on absolute precision in day and time, as stock prices fluctuate every second. The stock market is in part predicated on selling or buying not just on the right day, but at the right second of the right minute of the right hour. A second too late or too early in trading can mean the potential loss of large sums of money. It was the widespread possibility of loss of liquidity in a Y2K scenario that was troubling—if such a scenario could really take place, it would badly shake people's confidence in the entire stock market and financial system.

In banking, many big-ticket transactions like loans are linked to daily interest rates, such as the prime lending rate, which also fluctuates. In 1999 in Nigeria, the lending interest rate was 20.29 percent, compared to 17.80 percent in 1997, or 31.65 percent in 1993.

Many countries around the world took the coming of Y2K very seriously. In addition to worries about banks, and the possible inability to access funds, there were real concerns about other sectors as well, ones in which computer systems controlling critical infrastructure might fail, or fail in many sectors at once. Air traffic control was seen as very vulnerable. People also worried that the military would be unable to function; that power plants would fail, leaving entire regions in blackout; and that police, fire and emergency services would be hampered. A 1998 Gallup poll in the United States revealed that almost 40 percent of the public believed Y2K-related problems would last between several weeks and several months.

The atmosphere was fearful, and most people in banking were convinced that there would be some kind of computer failure. I wanted to be proactive, so I began to look for software Zenith could use that would see the bank into the New Year unscathed.

We found a brilliantly designed program that had recently been developed by Phoenix International in Orlando, Florida. Our first step required that I take about a dozen of my software and hardware engineers to Florida with me to meet with the company that had developed the software.

The senior-management team immediately made us feel welcome by personally meeting us at the airport. After taking a short time to refresh ourselves in the hotel, we began a series of extensive meetings, during which we got our first look at the new software. We were very interested in the demo we were given, and with what we learned about the front-end program interfaces and services as well as the architecture of the software design.

The Zenith computer team I had brought with me were—in my opinion—some of the most gifted software designers ever assembled. When they analyzed the Phoenix software, they decided to carry out a user-acceptance test on the program. Through this testing, they found some minor adjustments that would have to be made to accommodate our Zenith Bank modus operandi. My team had to stay in Orlando with the software manufacturers for an additional three weeks to run tests, while I returned to Lagos to run the bank. Ultimately, with all the bugs worked out, we had the product we needed. We signed a contract, and the Orlando team came to Lagos to install and implement the software.

One of our biggest and best-known clients of the time was ExxonMobil. They were so fearful that Nigerian banks would not prepare and avail themselves of the cutting-edge technology to make their systems Y2K-compliant, they told us they would prefer to move their funds to an American bank.

I told them that should our computers fail, Zenith Bank would pay for the damages of all their systems. I offered a guarantee of protection that, in effect, was 100 percent insurance. As a result, ExxonMobil agreed not to move their business out of Zenith.

It happened that January 1, 2000—the Y2K commencement—fell on a Saturday. No matter the outcome, it was a stroke of luck that Y2K was not on a business day. I went to my office beforehand and met with my software and accounting teams. One of our jobs was to send a current financial-account printout to ExxonMobil, However, my confidence was not as outright comprehensive as my offer suggested. Frankly, I had panicked and now had to be absolutely sure, viewing our system operations with my own eyes. At 2 p.m., the ExxonMobil team came by to check for themselves if our software had stood the test. Of course, it had—and we kept ExxonMobil's business.

In hindsight, Y2K is often described as much ado about nothing, the much-discussed Millennium Bug that proved to be more of a mosquito-sized glitch than an invading malfunction capable of taking down nations. *The Washington Post* estimates that the United States spent more than $100 billion to keep its systems safe from crashing; put simply, that equates to $365 for every person in America. Had the world overreacted? Had I? *The Post* asked US Commerce Secretary William Daley if the expense was justifiable. "Is this a lot of money? Absolutely," Daley said. "But the potential cost of not doing anything was far greater."

Certainly, finding and implementing highly rated software for a Y2K fix was costly to Zenith, both in money and in time spent. A business leader must not be afraid to spend money when it is prudent. There is an old saying—*an ounce of prevention is worth a pound of cure*. I think this is excellent as a business adage. Do what is best for your business today, but at the same time, be aware of what is coming down the line.

Most potential hazards do not make front-page news the way Y2K did, but somewhere they are always being talked about. If you always perform your due diligence, stay informed, and always look to the future, then you are in a position to anticipate the next glitch or crash or bug that could impact your business, and to trust that your gut will tell you whether you should be proactive, or ignore it altogether.

OUR LEGENDARY ZENITH
BANK CEO AWARDS

Start with good people, lay out the rules, communicate with your employees, motivate them and reward them. If you do all those things effectively, you can't miss.
—LEE IACOCCA, FORMER PRESIDENT AND CEO OF CHRYSLER

E very year in December, we compile a list of employees who had worked diligently in a variety of ways. What began as a tradition of public recognition and praise evolved over the years to more formal affairs. In December 2001, we held the maiden event of what was to become a widely loved and celebrated gala—the CEO Awards Ceremony. It was our intent to do something truly magnificent for our employees that year, so we planned an extravagant formal evening event. In the years to follow, the impact of these annual events would always prove to be long lasting, and collectively they have left indelible memories in the minds of many Lagos city dwellers.

Zenith Bank's first annual CEO awards gala was uniquely innovative and soon set the pace for others to follow. The sheer number and quality of Zenith's human capital was enough to generate a buzz. All of Lagos was agog with the glitz and excitement that the ceremony engendered. Far in advance of the event we already had lavish press coverage, and people in all circles—from social to professional—were full of expectations in the days leading up to the gala. No wonder it was soon dubbed the banking industry's equivalent of the Grammy Awards in Hollywood by social pundits.

In its subsequent yearly events, as founder and CEO, I spared no cost in ensuring that the awards and the celebratory after-parties would set a lofty standard in the world of business and entertainment alike. My event organizers, all Zenith staff members, were selected to form a committee charged with the responsibility of ensuring that the events were top-notch and seamlessly organized. Various subcommittees were set up to coordinate entertainment, invitations, logistics, and most importantly, the short-listing and final selection of the award recipients in the various categories.

The dress code of the awards was always tagged "Black-Tie/Evening Wear" to underscore the aura of class and sophistication associated with the event. It was not uncommon to witness an explosion of colors and stunning prints in the cutting-edge designs worn by the guests. In a local article written about the event, it was described in rich detail:

Every staff member, male and female alike, turned out in style. Ladies were adorned in gorgeous designer evening gowns by renowned designers such as Chanel, Diane Von Furstenberg, and Gucci, as well as couture outfits by acclaimed Nigerian designers Lanre Da Silva and Deola Sagoe. Of equal elegance were the ladies' diamond earrings and necklaces, Swarovski crystal jewelry and luxurious shoes and bags. Their hair coiffed to match their outfits, some undoubtedly sourced by personal shoppers and top-notch stylists from various cosmopolitan cities around the world; New York, Paris, and Lagos.

The gentlemen, not to be outdone, were dapper and debonair in their well-fitted tuxedos and dress shoes, as they cut the look of well-groomed perfection.

The beautiful and grandiose Civic Centre on Ozumba Mbadiwe, Victoria Island, was the venue of the awards. The event grounds, tastefully decorated with fresh flowers and plants, exuded an air of affluence and grandeur. Life-size backdrops and banners were placed strategically at all entrances, reception, and the two halls hosting the event.

The Red-Carpet event which preceded the awards was usually hosted in grand style by the crème de la crème of Nollywood, which added more spice and spritz to the occasion. The paparazzi were carefully selected to capture images of the occasion for the exclusive and private use of the bank, especially as this was a very private event.

Of course, the jewel in the crown of the evening was the presentation of the awards themselves. Prizes would be awarded to those who had proven themselves highly motivated and driven to achieve results beyond expectations. While the committee maintained a clear view of individuals' drive for excellent performance, it kept another objective in sight, which was to reward collective successes. To demonstrate Zenith's appreciation of strong leadership values, awards were also presented to various heads of branches, groups, and zones all over the various geographical regions where the bank has its operations.

The categories of awards presented to individuals included the following:

- Highest Demand Deposit Account
- Highest Fixed Deposit
- Highest Income-Making
- Best Marketing Staff (New Quality Relationship)
- Most Profitable Branch/Zone
- Most Improved Branch by Profitability
- Highest Public Offering (PO) Collecting Staff
- Most Outstanding Leader Award
- Most Outstanding Team Player Award
- Longest-Serving Staff
- Most Compliant Branch
- Best Fraud-Free Branch

The most deeply felt experience for me was greeting each award recipient with what came to be called the *golden handshake*. In my official capacity as founder and CEO of Zenith Bank, I shook the hand of each person who mounted the dais, and presented him or her with a beautifully crafted glass plaque inscribed with his or her name and the corresponding award title. Such a moment would be among the highest in the career of any Zenith employee. Most of these plaques still adorn the offices of various dedicated Zenith staff and are proudly shown to those who have joined the bank since the last MD/CEO awards took place.

Zenith Bank is one of the greatest success stories accredited to a pan-African organization. It is a globally recognized brand, recently named among the Top 500 Global Bank brands in the world. Zenith Bank has a well-earned reputation for recognizing and rewarding its staff generously, for it knows that these two incentives mean more to career-minded people than money. The unparalleled commitment and acumen of my staff is directly related to the fact that virtually every staff member of Zenith Bank, upon hearing about the yearly extravaganzas and seeing the awards, was motivated to strive to earn one of the prizes. It is widely known that recognition and intrinsic motivation are important to the success of most organizations, but the differentiating factor is finding ways to effectively devise and maintain a celebratory event that truly captures every facet of its people, from their wit and wisdom to their beauty in evening attire.

Some might wonder why I go through all the time and expense of throwing such a lavish event each year when I could host a perfectly nice evening for a fraction of the cost. I might first respond by pointing out that the meteoric rise of Zenith Bank from year to year is evidence of my success in championing an assertive style of management while cultivating a motivational climate. In other words, the proof is in the pudding. The real answer to the question is that there *is* a difference in going over the top with the awards ceremony—I do it to *show* my employees how proud I am of them, I do it to set the bar ever higher for them and for myself, and I do it to show them that I won't settle for less at their awards ceremony because *they* are worth so much *more.*

And I do it because it's *fun*, which is a very good sign. A happy business is a healthy business, so whenever you experience a sense of fun in your company or with your co-workers in general, take note. It's easy to look for signs we're doing things wrong, but it's just as important to notice the ones that tell us we're doing something right.

OWNER-PRESIDENT MANAGEMENT (OPM)

The future of tech will be written in Lagos, Nairobi, Kampala, and cities across Africa.
—JEREMY JOHNSON, ANDELA CEO AND FOUNDER

I n 2002, I was engaged in my annual attendance at the Owner/President Management seminar. Harvard Business School began this program forty years ago, and ever since, OPM has been offered to top businesspeople and entrepreneurs from all over the world. It's a three-week course of study, annually for three years, of both fundamentals and emerging trends in leadership in business and financial management, negotiation and strategy, and marketing/branding, taught in classroom-style courses by Harvard Business School's faculty. At this time, I was particularly interested in ways that people advertise materials and brand them.

In the three years that I attended the OPM program, one had to be in residence at Harvard University for the duration of each conference. In my first year attending we broke out into study groups, and I was required to make a presentation on the kind of banking business I had back in Nigeria.

That was a very important presentation. In my study group as I was preparing my presentation, I downloaded the Zenith Bank website. Not too many businesses in Africa had even rudimentary websites at the time. Working with some Zenith IT officers, I built a world-class website that displayed Zenith Bank's vision and mission, along with most of our products and services.

The site was truly dynamic, and it won awards as the best business website in Nigeria. I loved the website, which is interactive and was always at the top of any internet search. Viewers would type in questions, and the answers would load immediately. My OPM colleagues didn't believe it, but our information technology gave us the ability not only to build our website and brand our business, but to begin to change the negative perceptions people had of Africa. At first their comments and questions showed that they were coming from a very antiquated view of Africa.

Since our website had a venue for anyone to post questions, we were becoming accustomed to the degree of ignorance displayed about our country. The OPM attendees were not always innocent in this regard either. We even had to correct a few who thought Africa was one big country. I can tell you that it is quite troubling to be in the company of first-rate businesspeople from all over the world, and to find that more than one of them never knew Nigeria was a nation—one country of many on the African continent. More often in our discussions at Harvard, I was asked things like "What is the banking system in Africa?," as if Africa were a single country with one economy and currency.

I knew that the website would impress them, and it did—making it even more embarrassing to hear individuals theorize out loud that the website design and construction must have been shopped out to the US or the UK. Their reasoning was along the lines of "they can't do this kind of thing yet in Africa."

The truth is we can, and we have.

THE INITIAL PUBLIC OFFERING

*Great opportunities don't come every day—recognize them
and seize them with every chance you get.*
—MATT EHRLICHMAN, PORCH CEO AND CO-FOUNDER

I n 2004, the government of Nigeria declared that banks had to be recapitalized at a minimum of ₦25 billion— some $188 million—or be liquidated. This was a substantial increase from the two billion naira which had previously been the amount of capital required. The government's reasoning was that to avoid the rate of bank failure in the 1990s, banks must achieve a substantially greater liquidity to operate safely and with stability. Out of ninety banks in existence at that time, only twenty-five were able to raise sufficient funds to achieve recapitalization. Some avoided liquidation by merging four, five or even six other banks. This explains why only twenty-five banks independently survived. The rest either failed, or were swallowed up by other banks.

At the time of this writing, we have, in Nigeria, a total of only twenty-two commercial banks and five merchant banks.

Zenith Bank was one of only two banks that had no need to acquire or merge with any other financial institutions. Three of the older banks—First Bank, Union Bank, and UBA— had by virtue of longevity already achieved the ₦25 billion, but they moved to acquire other banks to significantly increase their size. When we announced an initial public offering (IPO), the public mood was extremely confident, and the demand for Zenith stock was so great, that our IPO was oversubscribed, which was very happy news. Luckily for us, we were able to raise ₦48 billion (at the time this was $360 Million)—though we were permitted to keep only one third of that sum—in accordance with the stock exchange rules. What was important was that we had survived the consolidations, we were healthy and growing by leaps and bounds, and we had the confidence of the Nigerian public.

How did we achieve this remarkable success when so many other banks couldn't? We adopted a specific and methodical approach using geographic and topographic mapping that allowed us to determine the distances between towns. The regional segmentation of those branches enabled us to assign marketing responsibilities to various regional sales teams whose zone head in turn apportioned targets to well-trained marketing officers. Each marketing staff drew up a comprehensive list of potential investors, some of whom had never bought shares of anything in their lives. The offices of these targeted potential investors were visited to discuss the intricacies of investing in Zenith Bank shares. Those marketing officers were promised the opportunity to receive some incentives by way of recognition, which would be commensurate with the number of shares each one sold.

Secondly, we contracted the professional services of agents with skills in advertisement, sales promotion, marketing strategy, and public relations. They designed various promotional materials including flyers, brochures, television ads, radio jingles, and newspaper ads—all to promote the sales of the Zenith Bank shares. Together with the promotional agents, we came up with the marketing campaign slogan: "From generation to generation"—the idea being that Zenith Bank shares (and by implication the excellent performance of Zenith Bank) would endure for generations.

Finally, the fourteen-year track record of Zenith Bank, having been in operation since 1990, was so impressive that very well-informed investors could not resist it and potential investors who were less-informed gravitated toward the excellent brand reputation of the bank. The institutional investors, fund managers, private equity investors, venture capitalists, and other investors all deserve to be recognized and appreciated for investing in the bank's IPO.

PHILANTHROPY:
THE JIM OVIA FOUNDATION

Philanthropy is not about the money. It's about using whatever resources you have at your fingertips and applying them to improving the world.
—MELINDA GATES, BILL AND MELINDA GATES FOUNDATION CO-FOUNDER AND CO-CHAIR

Throughout my career, my ambition has never been limited to business success and prosperity. I have always felt very strongly about my country and my fellow Nigerians, and believed that what success I could achieve should also benefit Nigeria.

In December of 2004, I established the Jim Ovia Foundation, a not-for-profit initiative with the goal of unlocking the potential of Nigerian young people. In Nigeria, more than half of the 182 million citizens are under the age of thirty, and more than 40 percent of the population is under the age of fourteen, creating a phenomenon sometimes called a youth bulge.

The foundation's mission is to invest in the unlimited and untapped potential of Nigerian youth as the key to socio-economic growth—to enhance the standard of living of the society, increase human efficiency, and equip Nigeria's young people with the necessary skills and training for leadership by fostering a society literate in information and communication technology (ICT). We are seeking to equip the future of our nation through the paramount avenue of education and ICT. The foundation's long-term goal is to bridge the knowledge gap to enable Nigerian youth to compete in a global economy and to incorporate ICT into the Nigerian education curriculum as a fourth science to ensure progressive and continuous learning.

Recognizing the link between lack of quality education and poverty, the foundation has embarked on the critical issue of closing the economic gaps created by these deficiencies. In an age when formal and digital literacy are entry-level requirements for most corporate positions, the breach between educational and digital literacy is widening. At the same time, lack of infrastructure and financing contributes to the decline in numbers of well-trained talent to support the business landscape.

I strongly believe that, ultimately, Nigeria's economic advantage and competitiveness will depend on equipping our Millennials with the necessary competitive skills. I have personally hired and trained the staff of the Jim Ovia

Foundation, and inspired in them a shared vision—to break the marginalization cycle of our country's underserved youth by means of ICT skill development, facilitating their integration into the formal labor market and competitive global economy. To accomplish these ends, the foundation engages in a number of philanthropic programs, including the Jim Ovia Scholarship, founded in 1998, to provide financial aid to outstanding Nigerian students, by way of funding the full duration of an undergraduate program. In establishing the scholarship, I hoped to create a network of future leaders within Nigeria who can compete globally with their peers, bring new ideas and creativity, and are committed to improving the lives and circumstances of people in their respective communities. Scholarships are awarded based on personal intellectual ability, leadership capability, and a desire to use their knowledge to contribute to society throughout Nigeria by providing service to their community and applying their talent and knowledge to improve the lives of others. Over time it was expected that the Jim Ovia Scholarship beneficiaries would become leaders in helping to address challenges related to health, technology, and finance—all areas in which the foundation is deeply engaged.

The Jim Ovia ICT Entrepreneurs Program seeks to empower budding entrepreneurs to tap into the emerging ICT market in Africa. The initiative seeks to nurture young entrepreneurs to their full potential over a period of twelve months.

A total of five to ten of the competitively innovative ideas are selected and funded with the goal of impacting fifty young entrepreneurs annually and selected applicants are trained by world-class professionals on developing mobile applications. In addition, beneficiaries are provided access to necessary training, counseling, and mentorship throughout the project cycle.

To date, 500 young people have been trained by professionals in developing mobile applications. Young entrepreneurs receive training in practical, technical, and entrepreneurship skills they will need to improve employability and job creation in the emerging ICT-driven market. This initiative hosts a software-application business forum, in which viable and innovative ideas are selected for funding. Selected beneficiaries are awarded up to $30,000 per idea.

Another program of note is Read-Up, an early intervention program aimed at promoting the tools and opportunities to empower the future of Nigeria. The objective is to assist marginalized youths between the ages of six and ten to become familiar with the digital age in a global environment by bridging the digital divide through ICT. Computer and technological literacy are essential tools for education, business, and communication in today's world. Those without access to ICT skills often lack opportunity and are therefore marginalized. With Read-Up, the digital divide is brought closer by providing training and access to these youths.

The Jim Ovia Foundation remains fully committed to continuing programs that nurture upliftment of underprivileged youth, and planting seeds for Nigeria's bountiful future.

BYOI: BUILD YOUR OWN INFRASTRUCTURE

I can't change the direction of the wind,
but I can adjust my sails to always reach my destination.
—JIMMY DEAN, AMERICAN SINGER AND ENTREPRENEUR

A s we continued to expand and open new branches, our size had become sufficient to see us getting ready to tackle some of the infrastructure decay directly.

To do business in Nigeria was to depend on the supply of power owned by an inefficient government monopoly then called NEPA (National Electricity Power Authority). Their electricity supply was unreliable. A popular joke at the time was that NEPA actually stood for "Never Expect Power Always." Any business wishing to computerize could not afford even a one-minute power failure. In fact, the lack of consistent 24/7 power from NEPA was a major factor in why other banks would not jump on the cyber bandwagon.

To achieve 100 percent reliability for our computer operation, we built our own source of electricity. We installed three giant generators at our main office, creating a daisy-chain of emergency support—the first generator would be backed up by the second generator, which would be backed up by the third generator—with only the fourth backup being the National Electricity Power Authority itself.

Another significant problem we were working to address was the matter of Ajose Adeogun Road in Lagos, on which our head office was located. Like many roads in Lagos, it was often flooded and was covered in potholes. Some people let us know they were afraid to come to our bank because of the damage that might be sustained by a car on our old road. I called a meeting with my bank managers, and presented the idea that since the government could not afford to fix every road in Lagos, we would simply have to fix the road to Zenith ourselves.

The process of rebuilding the road, which was three kilometers (two and a third miles) long, was very challenging. It was heavily used every day, so traffic was constantly passing during the construction. We widened it from two to four lanes, two for each direction. We employed traffic wardens to monitor and direct traffic flow while the work was underway. Sometimes we had no choice but to close down two of the lanes to work on them, after which we opened them to allow the traffic to flow again.

Meanwhile, we employed a landscaper to decorate the median by planting beautiful flowers and eventually palm trees. This served two purposes—it beautified the road making the drive more pleasant, and it also helped to mitigate the air pollution created by automobile emissions. Vehicle exhaust creates airborne-particulate-matter pollution—microscopic particles that can become trapped in the lungs of someone who is breathing by the road. Trees absorb the particulate matter. The US Nature Conservancy has reported that on average, the level of particulate matter in the air near a tree is reduced by between 7 percent and 25 percent. We were proud of our efforts for several reasons—they were good for business, they were good for our customers, and they were good for the air.

Given that the Ajose Adeogun Road had no streetlights, we decided to create a special effect by installing streetlights powered by our own generators. We contracted with electrical and mechanical engineers to install the lights as a standout feature of the road. When at last our repairs were complete, many more drivers started to use it, because it was well built and maintained, beautiful to look at, and flooded with light in the evening.

It was December when our newly repaired road reopened, and we thought people might appreciate some excitement during the Christmas season, so we added holiday decorations and strung colorful lights throughout the length of the road.

It was amazing to behold the lights winking and glimmering as the light of day faded. Many young people at home for their holiday vacation came to see the decorations, and some began to call the road the Champs-Élysées of Lagos.

As the decorations were so popular, we organized a Christmas parade, inviting students to participate—most of whom were from schools in Lagos and its environs. The Lagos State government issued a permit approving the cessation of traffic for about four hours on a specific Sunday, detouring the vehicles elsewhere, to make room for the beautiful Christmas parade. The parade was a huge success, and everyone who participated loved it. One group of students brought their instruments and played music, so in the end the Christmas parade became a street party. It was a great gift to see that once-decrepit street shining as if bedecked with jewels, and filled with the happy faces and excited voices of young people.

The new road became so popular that Kabiyesi, the Oba (traditional ruler) of Lagos, called me one day to thank me for the beautifully improved road. He is a very kind gentleman. He told me how he appreciated our various efforts in corporate social responsibility, and jokingly warned me not to contemplate changing the name of the road to Zenith Bank Street. I laughed and thanked Oba Kabiyesi for his fatherly advice, assuring him as a law-abiding corporate citizen that his command would be obeyed, and telling him, "Sir, I may have many ambitions, but they do not include having a street named after me or after Zenith Bank." The name of Ajose Adeogun has always brought the bank a great deal of good will and good luck.

It seemed everyone was pleased. As a result, the state government invited me to an appreciation ceremony and presented me with a certificate of concession to allow Zenith Bank to continue to maintain, as well as beautify, that road for the next thirty years. Zenith would happily ensure that the road remained in good repair, and a source of happiness both to drivers, and to the community at large.

The work of rebuilding and maintaining our existing infrastructure always seemed to lead to a new project. Another challenge was an inadequate clean-water supply, both at our headquarters and at other Zenith branches. Now that the road was in good shape, we realized it would fall to us to rebuild the infrastructure of the water supply. We commissioned seasoned engineers and contractors who were experts both in building and installing boreholes sufficient to supply water to all of our locations.

To this day I marvel at the difference our work made, both visible above the ground, and invisible in the water supply below. I was pleased that our renovations benefited not just Zenith but everyone, and that Ajose Adeogun Street went from being a source of irritation, car damage, and pollution to a source of beauty and connection from the bank to the community.

HARVARD LECTURE

For me, the winning strategy in any start-up business is,
'Think big but start small.'
—CARMEN BUSQUETS, CO-FOUNDER NET-A-PORTER

I n 2007, I was invited to give a keynote address for Harvard Business School's Ninth Annual Africa Business Conference, the world's largest student-run event focused on African business. The conference is held each year on the Harvard Business School Campus in Boston, Massachusetts. A wide range of people such as business leaders, educators, community leaders, and press, as well as African and African-American students attend the conference—some travelling from Europe or Asia to participate. The subject of my talk was the proliferating business opportunities in the African continent.

I began with an introduction, declaring that Africa is open for business, while displaying PowerPoint images of headlines such as *Bloomberg*'s "Africa Is Next Natural

Resources Hotspot, Morgan Stanley Says," and the *Financial Times*' "Nigeria May Be the Next Emerging Market's Gem." A great shift was underway; I pointed out, for example, that when I became the founding CEO of Zenith Bank, Nigeria was under a military government. General Ibrahim Babangida was the president and commander-in-chief of the armed forces and ruled the country for just over eight years. Since that time, political developments like the fall of the Soviet Union, advances in telecommunication, and reduced barriers to trade have accelerated economic globalization.

Ovia speaking at Harvard.

The global economy, I explained to the audience, was beckoning Africa, and in fact, Africa was already becoming integrated into the global economy—a trend led by banks. More than thirty African banks (including seventeen Nigerian banks) were already rated among the top 1,000 banks in the world. Furthermore, the African banking and financial system was already fully integrated and compatible with global-payments systems such as SWIFT payments, letters of credit, wire transfers such as Western Union, and others. Just the previous year, I added, a Goldman Sachs study on the BRICs identified Nigeria as one of the "Next Eleven" set of developing countries poised to join the largest world economies. That same study predicted that by 2025, Nigeria would be one of the top economies in the world, and by 2050 would surpass those of Korea, Italy, and Canada. A graph of the Foreign Direct Investment flow to Africa between 2000 and 2006 showed the amount of total foreign investment quadrupling to $40 billion in 2006, with more than $5 billion of that amount invested in Nigeria. Even more telling was the number of local investors bringing their own funds back into their native countries—always a key indicator of investor confidence.

One might ask what it would take, then, to realize the predictions of the Goldman Sachs study? I divided them into five categories for the audience—structural reforms, rule of law, privatization of industries, corporate governance, and political stability. In Nigeria, this would entail reforms in the banking and insurance sectors as well as the courts, and the implementation of digital technology to increase information sharing among government units handling customs clearance, imports, and exports.

If that sounded like a long list, I offered the reminder that today's challenges are always tomorrow's opportunities. Nowhere was that more evident than in Nigeria's information and communications-technology sector, which continued to serve both as a catalyst and a driver for development. Though significantly underinvested in the past, there were now huge investment streams pouring into the telecommunication sector, resulting in a 25 percent increase in teledensity in Nigeria. This is a tremendous rate of improvement for Nigeria, and one that had to continue if the rate was to meet the United Nations' International Telecommunication Union recommended level.

In the example of a sector development, such as telecommunications, I explained how a country's past failure to embrace technology was not necessarily an encumbrance going forward. In the year 2001, the number of fixed telephone-line subscribers in Nigeria remained the same, at approximately 240,000 lines. When mobile technology was introduced in 2002, the rate of subscribers increased substantially for each of the next four years, while during that time the number of fixed-line subscribers did not increase. This is what I call the leapfrogging of technologies, with the increasing internet penetration passing over the old fixed-line technology systems entirely, rendering the lack of fixed-line subscribers an economic redundancy.

Similar momentum could be seen in the financial landscape, with the rapid acceleration of the global fund flow that came about with the advent of electronic payments, plastic money, and debit/credit cards. The individual consumer, too, had often immediate access to funds and banking options through ATMs, mobile-banking technology, and internet banking. Of course, this kind of acceleration always gives rise to new pathways to fraud, most notably because of the opportunity to engage in "esoteric fraud," in which the perpetrator acts remotely and with some degree of anonymity. It is not without irony that the prevalence of this kind of esoteric fraud itself gives rise to new opportunities for development, in the research and software required to thwart it.

I closed my talk with a reminder that Africa is a land not only of huge potential, but tremendous opportunities and truly infinite possibilities. The advent of the internet multiplies those opportunities and potential many times over, now that Google puts a wealth of information at the fingertips of any African with a digital device and an internet connection. ICT advances make it possible for an almost immediate leapfrogging into the modern digital age, with wireless technology making the need for any substantial physical infrastructure obsolete. It might be difficult to imagine advancing to the forefront of the world stage so rapidly, I told the audience. It could happen, and in fact it had already happened.

When I started Zenith Bank, I reminded them, Nigeria was under military government, banking and telecommunication industries were solely under government ownership, and people were not confident about the economy. I put a picture on the screen of the very first Zenith Bank building in Lagos—a simple one-story apartment building. I said, "This was our bank. You can see how poor we were, and why we didn't have much likelihood of surviving. On a scale of 1 to 10, our chance for survival would have been barely a 2."

"We were not the only ones trying to stay afloat. Out of more than 120 banks, more than 70 percent had only received their banking licenses within the previous three years. There were no ATMs, no cell phones, or computers. Customers were lining up to do business with Zenith, and I saw we could make a difference. I was right. By 2004 we had a ten-story building all our own." When I showed that image, the audience got to their feet and cheered!

I told them how we helped changed the negative perception of Africa to something more positive and welcoming. I showed them the January 16, 1984 *Time* cover that featured a map of Africa and the headline "Africa's Woes: Coups, Conflict and Corruption." The feature article described

Nigeria as "a country of war and of hunger." Clearly, the Nigeria I had just described was a far cry from *Time* magazine's depiction.

By the time my presentation ended, I was confident I had done the job of challenging my audience to, "Talk about African opportunities!"

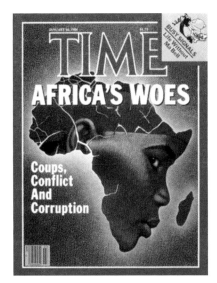

Time, January 16, 1984.

FOUNDING A MOBILE-TELEPHONE COMPANY: VISAFONE

It's not about ideas. It's about making ideas happen.
—SCOTT BELSKY, ENTREPRENEUR AND CO-FOUNDER BEHANCE INC.

The ascent or the arrival of mobile phones in Nigeria was more of a necessity than a desire, since Nigeria gained independence in 1960, it only had landline telephones, and relatively few of them. Telephone technology had existed in Africa since 1891, when the continent's first telephone service was established in South Africa. In 1956, the first co-axial submarine cables were run to Africa, connecting several countries. Nonetheless, intra-African calls were still difficult to make, and many had to be routed through Europe, making them very costly.

By 2000 there were some 400,000 fixed telephone lines in Nigeria. Nigeria's population at that time was about 120 million people, which gave a teledensity ratio of one line for every 300 people—painfully inadequate compared to other countries. Many people wanted telephones, but the government-run infrastructure was not expanding. Nigeria's 400,000 telephone lines were run through cables attached to telephone poles, with multiple lines crisscrossing the streets and buildings—both cumbersome and difficult to maintain. Telephones were also very hard to come by, and because of that they were a source of respect and power—if you had a telephone, you were a very important person. The government had the monopoly on running that infrastructure, it was important as a source of power and leverage, not as a profit-making industry.

At this time, mobile-phone technology was already being installed in some countries. Many European countries already had GSM (Global System for Mobile Communications) technology. GSM is a multiple-access technology that uses a time-division system, in which a caller's voice is compressed into digital data across three channels. Since compressed digital information takes up much less transmission space than voice data, three calls can be transmitted on the same band, with each call essentially using one third of the band capacity.

GSM technology systems were first shown in Africa in 1993 to Telkom in Cape Town. The following year, the first GSM networks were launched in South Africa by Telkom in partnership with Vodafone. Zimbabwe's Econet launched its own mobile network in 1998. Unfortunately, the Nigerian government was very slow in issuing mobile-phone licenses.

It was clear, however, that Nigeria both needed to make a quantum leap forward in teledensity, and that it was not going to happen through fixed-line expansion. It was necessary for us as a country to license mobile-phone companies. In 2001, the Nigerian Communications Commission awarded three mobile-phone licenses at a cost of $285 million each, with each company being required to provide 100,000 lines in the ensuing year.

Only three companies won the license—MTN, a South African-based company; Econet, a Zimbabwean company founded by Strive Masiyiwa, who organized a Nigerian consortium of investors to put money together to pay for the license; and Globacom, a Nigerian company founded by Mike Adenuga, a billionaire business tycoon. Later, a fourth GSM license was issued to an Abu Dhabi sovereign wealth fund called Mubadala Fund, who set up a mobile-technology company with a brand name of Etisalat which they had used in other countries in the Middle East, Asia, and Africa.

At that time, I did not think a GSM license would be worth the cost of $285 million, but I would soon realize my assessment was wrong, because the profit levels of these GSM companies were astronomically high. By the time I changed my view about the desirability of acquiring a license, it was 2008—putting me seven years behind the original groups. There was going to be a lot of catching up to do.

The government also allowed companies to operate within different regions of the country, using smaller-spectrum licenses allocated to regions in which they were permitted to operate. These were available at a fraction of the cost of the national GSM licenses, with the required investment closer to $4 million. Though far more affordable, those small-spectrum licenses restricted those regionals from operating nationally, meaning their radio wave would not transmit mobile-phone data across the country. Generally, these regional players were deploying a technology called CDMA (Code-division multiple access) to operate those mobile telephone services that did not enjoy the ecosystem of GSM.

To break into the mobile-tech sector, I had to consider the venture from a fresh perspective. Since the NCC restricted local investors to strictly regional operation, their networks could only operate in the small villages and rural areas of one of the 200 regions. With a signal of just 5 megahertz, transmission into another region was impossible, even if the regions happened to be compatible (which wasn't necessarily so). The result was that a significant number of these regional telephone companies began to fail. Hobbled with phones that would not work out of the immediate region, they could not make enough money to survive.

In business, it is crucial to be open to finding new approaches to the market, taking into special consideration what limits currently exist. Often the solution to bridging those limits is the key to the new approach needed. I could see that while the big GSM companies flourished, the small local companies could not compete, because their infrastructure was too tightly limited geographically. What if I were to acquire a series of these companies that collectively operated in a larger and more profitable territory? In 2008 I did just that, buying up several companies across the regions and combining them to be one large company. This provided me with 800 spectra, superior to the GSM network (the system used in Europe at the time—today all those technologies are integrated).

I decided to call my new company Visafone. I liked the idea that my phone company would give users access into other worlds, so when you made an international call you already had access to that country without physically going there. I first thought of using the word "passport," but it was too cumbersome. Then I focused on the word visa instead, combined with the phonetic "fone." Visafone—easy to say and remember, yet unique and edgy. It had everything.

When I had registered the company and completed my branding, I created and launched my website, which I then used to propagate the information highway. Unbeknownst to me, I was indirectly populating the vocabulary of Wikipedia, dictionaries, and Google—and all the other search engines in the world. When I did a search in Google for the name Visafone several weeks later, a miraculous 29,000 hits appeared. These inquiries all pointed a finger to one address: Visafone Communications, Ltd. in Lagos. It was tremendously gratifying to know I had created a name that had never existed before, and was becoming a household name, not only in Nigeria but in many other parts of the world.

NIGERIAN BANKING CRISIS

Never test the depth of a river with both feet.
—WARREN BUFFET, CEO AND CHAIRMAN BERKSHIRE HATHAWAY

I n September of 2008, Lehman Brothers—the American investment firm and global financial services company—collapsed, creating a chain reaction of bank failures. The crisis was predicated by countless loans for subprime (at high risk for default) mortgages, which were bundled and sold to various investors all over the world. These subprime loans were dependent upon an expanding housing market—the housing bubble—but there is a finite number of people at any given time who want to buy a new home, and a limit to how high the prices of homes could rise. When the housing bubble burst in the United States, the subsequent ripple effect spread to banks and other financial institutions across the world and caused monumental problems.

While New York was at the epicenter of the financial crisis in September of 2008, the ripple effect continued to spread outward in concentric waves, rolling through Ireland, Germany, and Greece, its momentum unchecked. It was only a matter of time until it reached Nigeria, where banks had recently had a series of public offerings and raised billions of naira from investors as far afield as Europe and America. When foreign investors and fund managers began selling off their investment in the wake of the Lehman Brothers collapse, the sell-off would include shares of all Nigerian banks.

The inevitable result of the selloff created a major financial tsunami in Nigeria, because the capital market as recorded in the Nigerian Stock Exchange lost about 50 percent of its value during the global financial crisis. Just as the US housing bubble burst, the bubble that had been created during the boom era of Nigeria's capital market had now ruptured.

More than 60 percent of Nigeria's banks at that time were less than fifty years old. Some of the bank owners lacked banking experience and their banks were badly managed. Those institutions were not only grossly undercapitalized, but their staff were not sufficiently trained to carry on operations as the crisis hit. Customers could not withdraw funds from some of those banks on demand. The result was catastrophic failure and collapse. The weaker banks in Nigeria whose shareholder funds evaporated with the value of their shares now went into a financial tailspin. When I was applying for my banking license, one of the newly established banks' shareholders and directors included two retired military generals, two traditional rulers, a trader who specialized in spare car parts, and a fish merchant. What truly distinguished this board was that there were no bankers or accountants on it at all, with the result being that the board meetings consisted mostly of arguing. They also would occasionally approve personal loans for themselves or their businesses— in one instance financing the shipping of a large quantity of a board member's frozen fish. When the ship sank in the high sea without adequate insurance, the result was a total loss, with the loan a huge write-off in the books. Such abuses violated the Central Bank's code of corporate governance.

In the case of the medium-strength banks, many depositors started to pull the plug by withdrawing their deposits. Capital is the lifeblood of financial institutions, and liquidity in the form of access to that capital is imperative for survival. For the banks whose liquidity virtually disappeared, it was a death sentence. I often tell my friends that liquidity to a business is like blood supply to a human. Everyone bleeds a little from time to time. When a human suffers an arterial wound, blood is lost on a massive scale in a brief amount of time, and if there is no means of staunching that wound, the ultimate consequence is death. Banks with liquidity could soldier on, but when access to liquid assets disappeared, the system collapsed.

The Central Bank of Nigeria governor at that time decided to help the banks by "opening the Central Bank vault" and giving those banks liquidity so they could stay alive. Even with that shot in the proverbial arm, some of the banks were too badly damaged to recover. Central Bank moved in and took them over—five in one day. They sacked the CEOs and board members and appointed new ones.

The government of Nigeria, through the Asset Management Company of Nigeria (AMCON) acquired the following banks:

- Afribank was taken over and the name changed to Main Street Bank, with the management duties passed on to AMCON on behalf of the federal government until its eventual sale to Skye Bank.

- Union Bank was acquired, and the name remained the same. It eventually was sold to a private-equity investor called Atlas Mara, founded by American Bob Diamond, former Group CEO of Barclays Bank PLC.

- Bank PHB was taken over and the resulting new organization named Keystone Bank Ltd. It was eventually sold to a pension-custodian company.

- Oceanic Bank was taken over, and the name remained until it was sold to Ecobank, who subsequently integrated the banks under the name Ecobank.

During this crisis period, Zenith Bank remained very strong and solid, because it had the largest Tier 1 capital (core capital by way of its shareholders), extensive liquidity (ready cash), the best asset quality (the aggregate quality of our loans), and a strong capital-adequacy ratio—the ratio regulators use to measure a bank's ability to withstand losses. In fact, Zenith Bank had such vast liquidity that it would have been sufficient to bail out as many as four banks, had we been called upon to do so. As it turned out, the Central Bank governor ordered the healthy banks in Nigeria, including Zenith, to begin to place deposits with other institutions that were not as healthy. This was a brilliant decision, for it enabled liquidity to resume circulation in Nigeria's banking industry. The purpose of this exercise was to allow all the banks in Nigeria to continue to operate and function normally, and to begin to lend money out, thereby growing the economy.

It was the same kind of move that occurred in American banking, when US Secretary of the Treasury Paulson created TAPA, which provided government money to the twenty-five largest banks in America, to ensure that liquidity was circulating in American banks and to encourage them to begin to lend money and grow the American economy. In the UK, the Bank of England did almost exactly the same thing as the American Treasury Department, by providing liquidity to banks such as Northern Rock, and taking over those that seemed too weak to save. For example, they took over Royal Bank of Scotland, and their total investment amounted to 80 percent of its equity. After about five years, the Royal Bank of Scotland, under a new board and new management who were appointed by the UK government through the Bank of England, once again became profitable. It was then ripe for the UK government to offer those 80 percent shares back to the public.

The banks that survived the global-crisis stress test in Nigeria, including those that were acquired and rebranded, went back to the drawing board to re-strategize about how to run their banks with more core capital and less risk. Some banks engaged the professional services of the Big Four auditors—PricewaterhouseCoopers, KPMG, Deloitte, and Ernst & Young—to present robust proposals of how to run their banks in a more sustainable, lower-risk, and profitable way.

Without a structured and prudent evaluation of risk, no business can ever be immune to the shockwaves of crisis. Risk is part and parcel of business only up to a certain point in testing the waters—but jumping into the river is likely to get you in over your head.

HOW WE EXCEEDED CUSTOMER EXPECTATIONS AND ACHIEVED SUPERIOR RESULTS

A satisfied customer is the best business strategy of all.
—MICHAEL LEBOEUF, BUSINESS AND MANAGEMENT AUTHOR

By 2015, we were one of the top banks in the country, and with our size and the respect and affection our growing customer base had for the Zenith Bank brand, we strategized about how to sustain our enviable position. Naturally, we would continue to work hard, but we needed to come up with additional strategies to become more efficient and drive our staff to improve their already-impressive productivity.

This was not a new impulse on our part—in fact Zenith employees were accustomed to my refusal to rest on my business laurels—success should never mean stasis. In any significant commercial venture, you're never done pushing, expanding, looking for new and better ways to do things. The task of building a healthy enterprise is never over. Larry Grove, the CEO of Intel, famously said, "Smart actions lead to success, but success breeds complacency. Complacency breeds failure, so constant innovation is a necessity. Only the paranoid survive."

As it's explained in the article "Inside Intel" from the *Harvard Business Review*, "... Grove believes that at least *some* fear is healthy, especially in organizations that have had a history of success. Fear can be a healthy antidote to the complacency that success often breeds. A touch of paranoia— suspicion that the world is changing against you—is what Grove prescribes."

Grove's management principles are, for the most part, very highly thought of in America's Silicon Valley. When Steve Jobs was struggling to come to a decision as to whether he should return to Apple, it was Andrew Grove to whom he turned for advice. In the 2015 book *Strategy Rules*, David Yoffie of Harvard Business School and Michael Cusumano of the MIT Sloan School of Management wrote about some core similarities in the three giant tech CEOs, Grove, Jobs, and Bill Gates. Those similarities include the constant push to expand, or find a way to do what they did well even better, and to expand the reach of their own business, not blindly, but in considering carefully what changes in the world and economy would entail—a characteristic described as "strategic foresight." Another similarity the book draws between the three is knowing how to "reason back"—to know what your customer base will need in a year, or in three years. Steve Jobs' strategic foresight was in designing computer systems that were easy to use, and down the line his reasoning resulted in products like the Macintosh, which arrived to consumers with all systems and programs already loaded. All the consumer had to do was open the box and take the computer out.

At Zenith, we've been doing similar kinds of strategizing and predicting consumer needs almost from the very beginning, most tangibly in our push to digitize our bank and all of its systems. We had annual planning meetings to pinpoint where it would be best and most appropriate to focus on change.

The first week of 2005, for example, we had a strategy session to expand our marketing goal, as well as to increase the revenue for that financial year. We held a kind of think tank for a new slogan, and ultimately agreed on "Surpassing Customer Expectations." Throughout the bank, Zenith's staff had the slogan affixed to their doors or displayed on their desks or hanging from their walls. The effect was that the real meaning of the words permeated employees' minds and became second nature. The intention behind the marketing words was internalized in every one of my workers.

In real-world customer relations, that slogan manifested in various ways in which we supported customer businesses. With ExxonMobil and Total Petroleum, for example, we visited their filling stations to collect and pick up their cash sales for each day. Nigerian businesses at that time were cash-based, and the means for money transfer was limited. There were no credit or debit cards, and in fact the use of cheques for purchasing petrol was unacceptable. After a few years, some other banks saw this as a means of gaining customer approval, and copied us.

Another way we surpassed customer expectations was by hand delivering all corporate customers their bank statement on the day it became available, the first of each month. Customers appreciated this service very much, because it was much more personal and effective than the approach of other banks, which delivered their statements through normal post office channels—where such statements took several days or even a week to reach the customers.

In 2006, we met again to determine where we might now focus in the wake of such success in "Surpassing Customer Expectations." Everyone had an idea or a suggestion, and what I began to hear was that anticipating what our customers thought they should *get* could be perfectly balanced by a focus on what Zenith employees thought they should be able to *do*. Our business slogan for that year became "Surpassing Superior Performance."

For the following ten years, we continued to devise these internal strategies, such as "Quantum Leap" and "Quantum Leap II." When we officially became both the largest in capital-base and one of the most profitable banks in Nigeria, we did not see it as an indication that we had successfully completed our marketing targets. I was determined, as Larry Grove might say, to avoid letting Zenith's success breed complacency. With every new height we reached in the business year, when the new year began, we'd go back to the drawing board for yet another mission statement that would reflect our position.

In the five years following the 2008 financial crisis, a number of Nigerian banks suffered liquidity crises which prompted the Central Bank to step in and rescue them. Despite the slowdown during that period, Zenith Bank remained solid, with robust liquidity. I felt it was a good time for me to take a break in my role as CEO, having per-sonally led and grown the bank for twenty years. I therefore retired from my position of founding CEO in July 2010. I then proceeded to establish Quantum Capital, a private-equity company that allowed me to begin focusing on real estate and other investment opportunities.

In July of 2014, I returned to the leadership of the bank as the chairman of the board of directors. On my return, I wasted no time in encouraging the staff, through the board of directors, to come up with a new mission statement that would guide us for the next five years. The chosen title was "Transformational

Growth"—because we saw that we needed to continually reinvent ourselves. That transformation has continued to the time of this writing.

CIVIC TOWERS

Real estate cannot be lost or stolen, nor can it be carried away. Purchased with common sense, paid for in full, and managed with reasonable care, it is about the safest investment in the world.

—FRANKLIN DELANO ROOSEVELT, FORMER US PRESIDENT

A recent study in China using data on per capita GDP and real estate investment found indications of "a significantly positive contemporaneous impact from real estate investment on economic growth"—findings that were true both for housing investment and commercial and business properties. I was well aware that in addition to being a historically excellent investment, real estate development in the right place at the right time would create numerous benefits, both directly and indirectly, to the surrounding community.

Real estate, as the old saying goes, is all about "location, location, location." It was clear to me that Lagos had enormous potential for a real estate investment. Lagos is not just the largest city in Nigeria, but the largest and fastest-growing city on the African continent, with a population of some 20 million people. A sea channel draining the lagoon into the Atlantic Ocean separates the island areas of Lagos Island and Victoria Island from the mainland. The word *lagos* is Portuguese for lakes, and originates from the name the fifteenth century explorer Ruy de Sequeira gave the area: Lago de Curamo. Today, Lagos is the thriving center for business, music, and finance as well as a tourist destination drawing visitors to its sandy beaches and lively nightlife.

The building complex, called Civic Towers, was being developed by Quantum Properties, which is a subsidiary of Quantum Fund Management Limited, a private equity company which I founded when I retired from being the CEO of Zenith Bank in July of 2010. I had already settled on a prime location on Victoria Island's Ozumba Mbadiwe waterfront, directly facing the mainland across the lagoon, as the site for this one-of-a-kind commercial office complex. Located at the intersection of Adetokunbo Ademola Street and the prestigious Ozumba Mbadiwe Avenue, Civic Towers was in the enviable position of occupying the epicenter of Lagos' business district. Real estate in an island metropolis is always at a premium—as in New York City, there is unlimited demand for a finite supply of land, and Victoria Island is akin to an African Big Apple.

Right: the Civic Towers at night.

The Civic Towers at night.

The Civic Center at night.

I held extensive meetings with the architects, and pinpointed the key elements I wanted my building to have—it should stand out, with features that were unmistakable, unique, and recognizable from any location or view, near or far. Several plans were drafted and submitted, and an architectural company's design won the day by virtue of the dagger-shaped communications tower atop the structure. The tower gave the building the distinctive silhouette that has made it the most iconic structure in the Lagos skyline.

The contracting bid was awarded to Cappa and D'Alberto PLC, perfectly qualified by their five decades of working experience on large-scale construction and tall buildings in Nigeria. Construction began in 2012, and Civic Towers was open for business by the summer of 2015. Within several months, the building achieved 100 percent leased occupancy to a select group of multinational corporate tenants and is currently the Lagos headquarters of the biggest corporate names in Nigeria, including the venerable accounting firm Deloitte, and global-technology giant Microsoft.

Every feature and amenity in the building was designed with a single standard—what does an executive who spends more than half of every day at the workplace most want in an office environment? As someone fitting that description, I knew what the answers were—strategic location with multiple avenues of approach; easy access to parking, dining, shopping, and entertainment; spacious offices with ten-foot-high ceilings and floor-to-ceiling double-glazed exterior glass to showcase the panoramic waterfront views.

The combined attraction of the Civic Center, which was built ten years earlier, and the Civic Towers provides a remarkable project masterpiece that has been called one of the best of its kind in Nigeria. The juxtaposition of the two is no accident—that design creatively capitalized on space so that the buildings would be connected by a luxury car park—with all three properties equipped with CCTV security cameras on the entire length and breadth of each perimeter.

Security is a priority in every aspect of the design, with on-site guards, secure perimeter doors, and after-hours entry functions utilizing card-chip technology. In addition, security personnel are stationed in the car park, who are available to escort individuals in and out of the buildings if they so desire.

Getting to the Civic Towers, one need not bother with the hectic Lagos traffic, because the location affords unique alternatives to road transportation. Visitors and corporate tenants can reach the Civic Towers by helicopter, private boat, or a ferry that operates from a waterfront jetty at the foot of the building.

At night, the communications tower is a luminous beacon, imposing and elegant. Drivers coming to the mainland from Lagos Island may catch sight of the tower as far away as the Third Mainland bridge, twelve kilometers to the north. Seen from a distance after sundown, the tapered blade of the tower gleams like a diamond against the night sky—it could be Dubai's Burj Khalifa or New York's Empire State Building.

Today, Victoria Island is in more demand than ever before, as evidenced by increasing numbers of new commercial buildings, hotels, and residential developments joining the skyline. I consider it a privilege to be a part of the growth of this great city. The Civic Towers means many things to me personally, but above all it is a living symbol of the heights we have reached, and of the bright future that lies ahead for Nigeria as we continue to rise.

NETWORKING, NETWORKING, NETWORKING

No man is an island entire of itself; every man is a piece of the continent, a part of the main.
—JOHN DONNE, BRITISH POET

anking is a business based upon trust and relationships. Customers were willing to place their money in Zenith Bank as a start-up in 1990 because of the relationships I had built with them over the years whilst working at IMB and Merchant Bank of Africa. I had built up a strong network of top corporate contacts that served as the pipeline for Zenith Bank's initial customer base. Our strapline has always been: people, technology, service. In the early years, I always made it a priority to personally interview the new professional staff, no matter how young they were. I sought to identify that extra spark that would drive their passion for embracing the Zenith culture. They would be on the frontline to drive the bank's network of clients.

This network of clients now spans three continents. I recognized early on the importance of networking internationally. Banking is a global business and thus it is important to be part of the global conversation. The World Economic Forum (WEF) is the preeminent arena for this dialogue. Established in 1971, the WEF is best known for its Annual Meeting in Davos-Klosters, Switzerland, an alpine village with a population of 11,000. For one week in January, over 2,500 of the world's captains of industry and heads of state descend upon Davos to discuss how to shape global, regional, and industry agendas. In the early days of the WEF, one needed to be introduced by an existing member to participate—one needed a network to network! Fortunately, the former Nigerian Interim President, Chief Ernest Shonekan, was willing to endorse me for my very first attendance. This was in January 1999. I was now attending seminars sponsored by Andy Grove, the founder of Intel; Bill Gates, the founder of Microsoft; and Larry Page, the founder of Google. In 2016, I was invited to be a member of the Community of Chairmen of WEF. In 2018, I was appointed as chairman of the African Regional Business Council of the World Economic Forum. As expounded later in the book, attending the WEF in Cape Town in 2015 enabled me to add Matt Lilley, the CEO of Prudential Africa, to my network of business contacts. The result of this meeting culminated in the landmark partnership between Prudential PLC, one of the world's largest life insurance companies and Zenith Life Insurance—Nigeria's fastest-growing life insurance company.

The next significant global discourse has the UN at its epicenter. The same group of heads of state and captains of industry convene in New York towards the end of September each year to attend the UN Meeting of the General Assembly. Its private sector counterpart is the UN Global Compact Group, which counts over 9,600 companies across 161 countries as its members. This group, which I am proud to be a part of, is the world's largest corporate sustainability initiative. Anchored around this event is the Clinton Global Initiative (CGI) and the Bloomberg Business Forum. The CGI had a unique appeal to me—they called for action rather than words. Each attendee was asked to commit to achieving a particular goal. I have always strived to ensure that Zenith Bank was a good corporate citizen and I now had the opportunity to push this aspect from an international perspective. In an emerging economy like Nigeria, the multiplier effect of job creation is in the double digits. Education and job creation are the key areas that I knew Zenith Bank could tangibly impact within Nigeria, and thus I focused Zenith Bank's and CGI's targets on same topic.

The impact of networking does not need to be on a global scale alone. However, one should not underestimate the hidden role luck has in business. Attending a small cocktail event in Lagos, I was introduced to CNN's representative in

Nigeria. I had been watching CNN's "Inside Africa" for some time, but I was not convinced that it should be sponsored by any African country. Angola was the sole sponsor before 2008. My view was that journalistic integrity would be better preserved if it were sponsored by a corporate entity like Zenith Bank or an international oil company (IOC) operating in Africa. Fortune was on my side as the CNN's representative advised me that the contract was due to expire on December 31, 2007. This discussion was in September 2007. It was agonizing to wait three months and hope that Angola's government may no longer be interested in renewing their contract or would simply forget to do so. I am very familiar with how some public-sector officials in developing economies and frontier markets operate; absolutely not like the private-sector entrepreneurs who are viciously competitive and combatant by their everyday training. Their survival instincts cannot be matched by the best of public-sector modus operandi.

In the meantime, I prepared a proposal for the sponsorship of "Inside Africa" that was agreed in principle. My strategy was twofold: I wanted to showcase Zenith Bank on a global network of CNN's caliber and I wanted to encourage more positive stories about the continent. For too long, the narrative of Africa had been war and famine, conflict and poverty. With a population of one billion, I was confident that CNN could find enough content that reflected the aspirational, energetic, and groundbreaking entrepreneurs that Africa embraces. From the first African woman to win the World Boxing Council gold title (Catherine Phiri from Zambia), to Afrofuturism and the struggles of Nomads in the Sahara, to Kenya's ballet prodigy—one simple networking event helped redefine the narrative of what CNN reports on Africa globally. Those who were working with me closely on this project, both within Zenith Bank and CNN, will recall the phone call I made to them on January 1, 2008—not just to wish them a happy New Year—but to see if the Angolan CNN contract had been renewed or was it unencumbered for me to grab. Fortuitously, the "Inside Africa" sponsorship was offered to Zenith after signing an exclusive, multi-year contract. This is the type of deal that could only be "made in heaven."

Doing business in Nigeria is not for the faint hearted. The most important aspect is to get the right partner. With the thirty-first largest GDP in the world, and one of the fastest-growing economies, Nigeria was at the forefront of most international investors' destination list. In April 2018, I had the honor of attending the Commonwealth Business Forum in London. I was part of a panel where we discussed "Fintech" and the "Economic Collaboration Between Commonwealth of Nations." Whilst all the countries of the Commonwealth may share a common language as former colonies, I joked with the audience that the wealth wasn't in fact common! Having been the first new-generation Nigerian Bank to meet the stringent requirements to be granted a UK banking license, networking in the UK is key. Banking is not a carbon-copy cut and paste business: the strategy we adopted that drove our success in Nigeria will not work in one of the world's most developed financial markets. However, irrespective of country, culture, or religion—one aspect of banking remains consistent—the importance of relationships and networking.

All work and no play makes Jack a dull boy. My belief has always been that networking is not a ring-fenced activity tied to specific fora. Moreover, it is an activity that is incorporated in each day of an entrepreneur's diary. I will share some of my networking experiences at a few of the Olympic games. I have been fortunate to attend the five of the last six Olympic games: Atlanta, 1996; Sydney, 2000; Athens, 2004; Beijing, 2008; and London, 2012. In Atlanta, we were privy to watch the Super Eagles, Nigeria's national football team, win a gold medal against the soccer grandees of Brazil and Argentina. In Sydney, it was touching to learn that the Aborigines were settlers from Africa that had traveled there via Asia some 70,000 years ago. In Athens, we rented a family's primary residence—long before the days of Airbnb! In Beijing, the marvel of about 100,000 people acting as tourist guards for Olympic guests was marginally offset by the arrest of our own escort. Apparently, it was illegal to try to buy or sell extra tickets and the poor chap was detained for trying to buy extra tickets on our behalf until the end of the games. As global integration intensifies, the ability to resonate with people of different cultures, religions, and socioeconomic backgrounds is a vital ingredient for business success.

JAMES HOPE COLLEGE: EXCELLENCE AND EMPOWERMENT

Education is the most powerful weapon
you can use to transform the world.
—NELSON MANDELA, FORMER SOUTH AFRICAN PRESIDENT

I n 2010 I met with leaders of the community in my childhood city of Agbor, in Nigeria's Delta State, about a vacant empty lot. I was very interested in developing a project that would put the land to good use for the community. The officials were open to anything I had in mind, and suggested some kind of factory that would provide jobs to the local residents. I was already very clear about which people I imagined harvesting the fruit of this project. Throughout my career, I have continually sought to better the lives of the youth of Nigeria—and I was more committed to that work than ever. I told the community leaders my plan; I wanted to build a school.

In the wake of Nigeria's exponential population growth, some 45 percent of Nigerians are the under the age of fifteen.

Of primary school-aged children, 40 percent do not attend school. Schools can be few and far between in some areas, and families often need their children's help at home, or cannot afford the cost of uniforms and textbooks. As the youth population continues to grow, the demand on the existing schools and teachers is greater than ever, resulting in classes of up to a hundred children for one teacher in a rundown classroom without proper facilities. What is most needed as of this writing is immediate resources—new schools, more teachers, and programs to subsidize education costs for those who need it.

The Nigerian government stepped up and initiated a 2004 Universal Basic Education Act, establishing compulsory and free education. The problem is continuing to become more severe. In 2017 the Education Ministry acknowledged that Nigeria has the largest number of children in the world who are not being educated. On a recent trip to Nigeria, education activist Malala Yousafzai met acting president Yemi Osinbajo and asked him to declare what she called "an education state of emergency in Nigeria."

At my non-profit group, the Jim Ovia Foundation, we are keenly aware of what statistics show— that lack of access to quality education is a primary cause of unemployment and crime rates. For this reason, the foundation took on the work of impacting young Nigerians at a pivotal point in their mental development—the secondary school level. For all these reasons, I decided to build and fund a new school in Agbor, which would offer a world-class education for a subsidized fee, and with numerous scholarships made available. The new school would be built on the site of my old primary school that had been demolished many years earlier.

There is a story behind how the project came to be named James Hope College. The name James is my own, the one with which I was baptized. The name Hope came from an unexpected place. It was 2015; I was one of numerous people watching a stunning news broadcast from Chile, where thirty-three coal miners had been trapped far below the surface for two months. Surface-to-mine communication had just been established, and for the first time the miners were able to communicate their situation and their wishes. At the moment of the broadcast, a harrowing rescue effort was beginning, live on camera. A reporter said the wife of one of the trapped miners was due to give birth to a baby girl. Fearful of the possibility the father might not make it out alive, a fiber-optics line was provided to him. I remember being glued to the television with my wife as we watched CNN's minute-by-minute live coverage of the trapped miners. One story in particular struck a chord with me:

Ariel Ticona was able to pass a message to his wife, Elizabeth Segovia, following the birth of their daughter, using a fibre optic video link set up between ground level

and the small underground refuge where they could remain trapped for several months.

"Tell her to change the name of our daughter ... and give her a long-distance kiss," he said, as other miners shouted, "We're going to name her Esperanza."

Esperanza. Spanish for Hope. That single word expressed what those miners and their families and everyone following their plight were holding onto. Across the world, people focused on the miners and joined the massive expression of hope. It was a feeling that became even more poignant when every one of the miners was pulled to safety and reunited with their loved ones.

I was moved very deeply by Ariel Ticona's act, sending his message out through several thousand feet of earth with his daughter's name—such a positive, uplifting expression in a long dark night of crisis. The broadcast coincided with my thinking about what to name the new high school. The old primary school that had been demolished happened to be the very one in which I learned to speak English and to write my letters and numbers when I was five or six years old. The old structure had been completely demolished, and there was nothing in the place where the building had stood fifty-eight years before. In fact, an entire forest had grown up where it had once been. How extraordinarily fortuitous that the people of the village wanted me to build something on that

Left: James Hope College building.

site for them. The neighboring people were so poor they never imagined a former student might one day make enough money to build a new school. They had felt no hope of rising above their circumstances, and no reason to think they ever would have hope. Some five decades later, I wanted to give it to them. That is how the school came to be called James Hope College.

Today, the buildings of James Hope College stand on the lost foundation of my old school. The school is equipped with classrooms, science laboratories, and a great hall, and already has international standing owing to its high standards. At this writing, the current student population is 205—102 girls and 103 boys. Out of this number, seventy-six students, or about 35 percent of the enrollment, are on scholarship. Every student who attends this college will leave it with significantly improved prospects. Some will go on to college and graduate school, and to the most respected and exciting professions in the country. While it is only one school—a drop in the bucket of Nigeria's educational situation, it is more than that for Agbor, and for the many students who will win scholarships to attend—for them, it is the only school that matters—the school of Hope.

Right: James Hope College building with students and faculty.

NOMINATION AND APPOINTMENT OF THE CENTRAL BANK GOVERNOR OF NIGERIA

One of the truest tests of integrity is its
blunt refusal to be compromised.
—CHINUA ACHEBE, NIGERIAN NOVELIST

The Central Bank of Nigeria is headed by the Central Bank Governor (CBG). The Central Bank undertakes monetary policy in order to maintain Nigeria's external reserve, to safeguard the international value of the legal currency; act as banker and financial advisor to the federal government of Nigeria; act as lender of last resort to the banks; and to promote and maintain monetary stability and a sound and efficient financial system in Nigeria.

Given the utmost responsibility of the Central Bank, as headed by the CBG, it is obvious that the individual who is nominated and appointed as the CBG must be a person of certain requisite qualifications. The qualifications, therefore, are as follows: they must be a university graduate with a degree in economics and/or finance and banking and they must have achieved several years of banking or finance-related work experience. Of the past six CBGs, five of them have attained the level of managing director of their respective banks before being appointed. For example, the current CBG, Godwin Emefiele, was the managing director and CEO of Zenith Bank, a position he held for four years before his appointment. His predecessor, Sanusi Lamido Sanusi, who is now a traditional ruler, the Emir of Kano, was the managing director and CEO of First Bank before his appointment to act as CBG between 2009 and 2014. The question now is, how are these brilliant individuals chosen to be CBG?

Given the qualifications enumerated above, the president of the country has absolute prerogative to nominate a candidate for CBG, but that particular candidate must be approved by the National Assembly. The presidential officials meticulously review and evaluate every resume submitted. Of the many hopefuls, a handful of the most exceptionally qualified candidates—generally no more than five—are chosen for the shortlist. At this stage, candidates will be assessed on a personal as well as a professional basis. This personal assessment will require that a candidate demonstrates the highest levels of probity—a person of unequivocal integrity and impeccable character. They should not have any instances of personal or business bankruptcy, and any criminal record whatsoever is an automatic disqualification. Individuals who meet these criteria and demonstrate an overwhelming superiority in the professional realm are invited to attend a series of interviews which become the basis for the final decision-making process. This level of due diligence helps to ensure that the very best candidate is chosen for this highly important position. Once appointed, a CBG serves a five-year term.

I was particularly excited and pleased when the appointment of our current CBG, Godwin Emefiele, was announced in 2014. Godwin Emefiele had earlier succeeded me in July of 2010 as managing director of Zenith Bank, when I retired as the pioneer CEO of the bank. He managed Zenith for four years before he was appointed CBG. Having supervised him for several years, I was confident that he would consistently maintain a high level of professionalism and exemplary leadership skills. I was equally confident he would discharge his duties as CBG in a very responsible manner.

HOW AND WHY MTN
BOUGHT VISAFONE

Don't be afraid to give up the good to go for the great.
—JOHN D. ROCKEFELLER, FOUNDER OF STANDARD OIL

F inancial markets can move very fast anywhere on the globe—there is no such thing as "African time" in business. Nowhere was this more evident than in the competitive landscape in Nigerian telecommunications, which was evolving rapidly. Due to my experience, I could draw clear parallels between the evolutionary trajectory of the banking industry, and that of telecoms.

The original telecommunications ventures were incredibly profitable, but nonetheless, I spotted a huge gap in the marketplace, and established Visafone by acquiring and merging three existing mobile telephone companies. Visafone had adopted CDMA technology, the US technology adopted by Verizon and Sprint. The battle between CDMA and its

European rival, GSM, was akin to the VHS-versus-Betamax conflict of the late 1970s and early 1980s—and of course the *ultimate* victor in that competition was DVD.

At the time, CDMA had the significant advantage of being a lower-cost technology to deploy. However, this advantage was counteracted by a weaker ecosystem: handsets were network specific, costlier, and offered less choice. It was the classic trade-off—buy a more expensive handset to start with, and have lower-cost calls over the long term. CDMA operators therefore had to acquire handsets for their subscribers, which gulped up large amounts of capital in an already hugely capital-intensive business.

As with the decimation of audiotapes by CDs, a new technology was set to converge both CDMA and GSM—namely, LTE. LTE stands for Long Term Evolution—a name that did not describe the technology so much as its path-surpassing 3G technology. Positioned to be a game changer, the new broadband technology kid in mobile-network town was a data-heavy consumer of telecom bandwidth, and as such required large amounts of spectrum. Poising Visafone to gear up for this next wave of competition, we acquired more bandwidth. We had 10 megahertz of 800Mhz spectrum and an option on 10Mhz more. When I had my strategy team outline the business plan for the next five years, it became clear we would have to invest more than $500 million in the network to deploy this new technology and remain competitive.

As the founder of a major bank, I was acutely aware of the equity/debt trade-off. Telecoms had become a low-margin commoditized business, for essentially the same reasons desktop and laptop companies did. With several companies offering similar products and performance, the only feature remaining distinguishable is often the price—as prices dropped, so did the profit margins. In addition, the exchange rate was under pressure. One hundred percent of Visafone's cash inflows were in naira, so the $500 million would have to come as equity and from funds generated by the business. As an emerging market investor, you need returns of more than 20 percent per annum. I just couldn't see the business achieving that.

Meanwhile, competition in the mobile-phone industry had become cutthroat, creating a bloodbath. Profits had been sacrificed at the temple of subscriber numbers. Many operators were on a mindless quest to attract millions of low-end subscribers, even if they were not profitable. The market had been irrational for quite some time—and irrationality can outlive capital. My business philosophy had always been to be a market leader, not a follower. In the David and Goliath marketplace that had engulfed Nigerian telecoms, even my $500 million investment could leave Visafone a mere spectator in the industry amphitheater.

Whilst analyzing this with my strategy team, my Visafone rang. It was the CEO of MTN, Nigeria's 800-pound gorilla of telecoms. He was requesting a meeting, a confidential one. I accepted, and invited the caller to my home for the meeting. My home is both a sanctuary and a support office—the notion of a work-life balance has always been alien to me. Work has been my life and my life has been driven by my work. An entrepreneur does not have the luxury of switching off at 5 o'clock. In fact, many of my most important meetings were held late into the night. The relaxed setting of my personal residence has played host to CEOs, business leaders, and diplomats.

From financing to restructuring to approving, the role of the commercial banker is critical to the success of any deal. In my capacity as former CEO of Zenith Bank, almost every major mergers and acquisitions transaction crossed my desk. The combination of gut instinct and years of experience had empowered me with a savant's view of what constituted a good deal—and conversely what would be consigned to the trash-heap of failure. MTN was the largest telecom in Nigeria, while Visafone was one of the smallest. MTN was approaching me with an offer to acquire Visafone in its entirety.

I had never sold businesses before, only acquired them. I had nurtured every one of my companies from the cradle, building every business from scratch, and imbuing each with my blueprint for success, regardless of its sector. I had reaped the benefits via the dividends that each one of those companies had paid out. It felt as if we had just started Visafone, and watched as the company started to take its first major steps into the big league, with 2 million subscribers and growing. Visafone operated globally, employing some 2,000 staff and occupying eighty mini-shops and retail outlets. I was emotionally invested in the success of each and every business line—each and every employee, and each and every business decision that affected them.

I had to set my emotions aside. MTN knew I had the resources at my fingertips to continue to drive Visafone forward. The only reason I might consider selling, they reasoned, was if the price tag was enough to justify my parting with the business, the staff, the stake in the industry, and with the spectrum itself. Operators know that spectrum is a very scarce commodity—it is the artery that pumps their calls—and hence their revenues—across their networks. Many operators had gone bust through overzealous bidding for additional spectrum. So MTN knew that to avoid a bidding frenzy amongst their competitors they would have to make an exclusive offer with a purchase price so substantial it would be difficult to refuse. That is exactly what they did.

I set my private-equity company professional team on the numbers to confirm what I intuitively sensed—that this was a good deal, and more importantly a good deal that would reach financial closure. I have seen many deals that look good on paper still fall apart at the last minute, usually owing to issues of the ego. Was MTN the right fit? What about the softer issues? Subscribers had bought into Visafone because my name stood behind the brand—what would happen to the subscriber base once they were engulfed by the 800-pound gorilla?

Telecom companies are not bought and sold every day, and this fact remained in the forefront of my mind. My team remembered the Jim Ovia golden rule that you only get what you negotiate, and they negotiated very hard. This was not an offer I went out and looked for, but nonetheless it was in front of me—ever the dealmaker, I wanted an extra 10 percent on top of the existing valuation for all the sweat equity I had invested in the business. The deal was inked, and we managed to close in record time.

The unfolding of this offer and the ensuing negotiation happened against the backdrop of MTN suffering one of the world's largest-recorded regulatory-imposed fines: $5.2 billion (this was later negotiated to a significantly lower amount). As a result, the entire MTN team changed midway through the sale process, necessitating our getting an entirely different group within MTN on board with the acquisition whilst they were distracted grappling with how to meet the $5.2 billion fine.

The intrigue wasn't over. To complicate matters, the Abu Dhabi-based sovereign-wealth-fund-backed operator called Mubadala, which owned the Nigerian mobile telephone company Etisalat, had learned of our impending deal. Recognizing the asset gold mine that Visafone owned, Etisalat sued

both MTN Nigeria and Visafone, as well as the regulator—
the Nigerian Communication Commission—for approving
the deal. Etisalat claimed that MTN was already too big and
dominated the market, and that the government should not
allow MTN to become bigger by acquiring Visafone.

The lawsuit was filed at the Federal High Court in Lagos.
The court's ruling was simple and straightforward: Etisalat
lost. Subsequently, a friend of mine called and commented
that the owners of Etisalat should spend more time learning
how to run their mobile-phone company. If they didn't do so,
he said, they might face a big financial problem. My friend's
comments proved prophetic. Etisalat could not pay their
overdue bank loans, and all the bank creditors formed a
syndicate to force the company to pay them. At the time of
this writing, Etisalat is still in default, as those bank loans
have not been paid.

Despite all these hurdles, I am proud to say that the deal
closed, and every one of the 2 million Visafone subscribers
enjoyed a seamless migration to the MTN network.

WORK/FAMILY ETHIC OF
AN ENTREPRENEUR

No matter what your career goals are, try to do
something different each day. See where it takes you, and
what you can learn. This has made every day of my life an
adventure—who knows where it might take you!
—RICHARD BRANSON, FOUNDER OF VIRGIN GROUP

Much has been written about the importance of a healthy work-life balance in business, whether for those starting businesses, working their way up the ladder, launching entrepreneurial ventures, or leading large corporations. An internet search on the topic will bring up scores of articles with titles like "Six Rules of a Healthy Work-Life Balance" and "Ten Steps to Achieve Work-Life Balance," some arguing that it isn't "balance" you need at all, it is "harmony" between office and home that should be the goal. Some of the articles concede that today, the ease of communication technology provides has blurred the lines between office and home. E-mails can be sent at any hour of the day or night, a practice sometimes seen as intrusive, yet the choice lies with the recipient as to whether to check e-mail at all outside of business hours.

But the entire question of this elusive "balance" between work and life poses a one-size-fits-all query to a no-two-people-are-the-same topic. Can there really be six rules of work-life balance that apply both to a junior salesman at an automobile company who hates his job, and a young lawyer who has just gotten a job at the firm he's dreamed of working at for years? I also don't think the presumption that "work" and "life" are at opposite ends of the spectrum for everyone. Is a writer only a writer while writing, and a different person in private life, or are the two inextricably entangled? I believe that for some people, their work is a central part of their persona; for me, that is absolutely the case.

I'm an entrepreneur, which in the very simplest terms means that I look for opportunity everywhere, and that I have an uncanny knack for finding it. It is a quality I was born with, which means my becoming an entrepreneur was an absolutely natural function of who I was and am, just as a fast, powerful, and competitive person might naturally become an athlete. Just as an athlete takes pleasure in being physically active, I take pleasure in engaging my mind in entrepreneurial ways. My work is never something I want to leave behind me in a darkened office at dinnertime.

Right: Ovia's daughter's wedding at The Savoy, London. L-R: daughter Tito, Jim, son Tomi, wife Kay, daughter Isioma, son Jesse, and daughter Ekene.

Home is both a place of peace and respite and a source of support outside of my office. Work has always been central to my lifestyle, and I neither can nor want to create any absolute barriers between the two. In my professional life, I interact with people all over the world from every time zone. It is just as likely for my important business and conferences to be conducted in the dark hours of the night as it is for them to occur in bright midday hours.

I have always felt it was important to take time to relax and spend some hard-earned dividends on a little good, old-fashioned fun. After finishing my MBA, it was Lagos that many of my friends and I went to work. Back then we called ourselves the Lagos Boys, named for the place we knew we could both come and work, and enjoy a social life. In the early 1970s when I got my first job as a bank clerk in the good old days of Barclays Bank, my friends and I used to take the public buses (LMTS) everywhere we needed to go. After work, sometimes we would go to Fela's Afrika Shrine (the original one) where you could eat snacks and listen to musicians like Fela Ransome-Kuti—the Afrobeat King—whose album *Shakara* was a national sensation. Sometimes we'd go to Bar Beach instead, just to sit and work while watching the water and listening to the waves. Lagos always was and still is a business center with all the associated hustle and bustle, but with the added benefit of any dining or entertainment experience one could desire. Fela Kuti's children built the

Left: Sports Day at Harrow School for boys, London. 2015. Ovia with his wife Kay and sons Tomi and Jesse.

New Afrika Shrine on the site of original venue, where I can be reminded of the good old days by listening to his son, world class musician Femi Kuti, performing several days each week. For those who prefer simple relaxation by the sea, Bar Beach remains Lagos' most popular oceanside spot, while boat enthusiasts can enjoy the Lagos Yacht Club, or the Civic Center's luxurious Aquamarine Boat Club.

It is likely that the distinction between office and home will continue to blur as technology enables more people to work on the go, without the old reliance on a physical workplace. To the extent that one can derive authentic pleasure both in the workplace and at home, I believe the marriage of the two can be a happy one.

It certainly is for me.

Above: Speech Day at Harrow School for Boys, London, 2015.
Ovia with his sons, Tomi and Jesse.

PRIVATE-SECTOR HEALTH ALLIANCE

It will take a movement, a public private coalition, to extract synergies and transform health outcomes in Nigeria.
—ALIKO DANGOTE, DANGOTE GROUP OWNER

Since my earliest encounters with computers in the mid-1970s as a college student at the University of Louisiana, Bill Gates has been someone I've admired and respected, as an innovative software genius, as a global business scion, and as a philanthropist. Many people are familiar with the work of the Bill and Melinda Gates Foundation and its role in improving healthcare and reducing extreme poverty globally. With lifetime-to-date donations exceeding $30 billion, Bill Gates is arguably the greatest philanthropist in the world, his generosity rivalled only by that of American business magnate, Warren Buffet. Many years later, when Bill Gates asked to meet with a small group of Nigerian entrepreneurs, myself included, it was as fellow philanthropists that he approached us.

As the most populous country in Africa, and the ninth most populous country in the world, Nigeria's 185 million citizens have faced a challenge in obtaining access to adequate health care. Given the surge in the population, infants and children have carried a heavy burden as a result, vulnerable to many preventable diseases and chronic conditions.

Across many administrations, the Nigerian government has worked to address issues affecting the poor, as evidenced in the National Economic Empowerment and Development Strategy (NEEDS) in 2004, and more recently address-ing health care specifically, with the Nigerian Health Act (NHAct) and the Basic Health Care Provision Fund, created to match financial resources with systems designed to improve the primary health-care system. Because of these long-term efforts, Nigeria increased the per-capita amount spent on health care by 103 percent over a thirteen-year period, from $102 in 2000 to $207 in 2013.

When policies and programs result in significantly improved statistics, there is always the danger that some com-placency will follow in the form of inaction—with no one more vulnerable than Nigeria's children. According to the World Bank's 2016 estimation, 44 percent of Nigerians are fourteen years of age or younger, meaning some 80 million Nigerian children at risk—a staggering number by any accounts.

Recognizing the urgency of those statistics, several of Nigeria's most successful business leaders and entrepreneurs believed—as I did—that government cannot and should not be the sole entity trying to solve societal problems. I had felt for a long time that the private sector must play its own role in devising such solutions. In my mind, it is quite logical—it is the private sector that creates most new jobs, and facilitates new opportunities and innovations—therefore the private sector needs to bear some of the responsibility for getting Nigerians access to quality subsidized education and effective health care. In doing so, they not only take care of their workforce, but they also take care of the workforce of the next decade, and the next, and the next.

I knew, of course, that the Bill and Melinda Gates Foundation continued to do an enormous amount of work addressing global health-care issues, and that these issues were the reason behind this particular visit to Nigeria. I met Bill Gates for the very first time in 2004, after I got on a plane in Lagos and flew all the way to Vienna for the sole purpose of hearing him speak at a conference. Little did I know that one day he would come to my country to meet with a hand-picked group of executives, and I would be one of them.

I was, of course, quite pleased when I was invited to take part in a discussion Bill Gates was hosting in Abuja in 2010. The meeting took place at the Hilton Hotel. Bill didn't beat around the bush—he'd asked us to the meeting, he said, because he hoped we would agree to create and set up a philanthropic organization that would serve as a private health alliance focused on Nigerian health care and health issues. He also spoke very movingly about his vision of eradicating polio and other serious but preventable health conditions in Nigeria. He believed that in Nigeria, this vision could be best served by Nigerians—men or women who are local to this culture and also visible and trusted both in Nigeria and abroad. People like us. If we were amenable to doing that, Bill told us, he would commit to helping support our group personally and financially, tripling our collective donations. Few would be surprised to learn that we agreed. We would not have a public face—or the name Private Sector Healthcare Alliance of Nigeria—for several more years. Nonetheless we *were* now part of a private-sector health-care alliance, our founding members including Aliko Dangote, Dr. Muhammad Ali Pate, Aigboje Aig-Imoukhuede, Sola David-Borha, and myself.

It was clear that our first mission must be to follow in Gates' footsteps and join his efforts to eradicate of one of the most damaging vaccine-preventable contagious illnesses in Nigeria and in the world at large—polio. The Gates Foundation had been sending immunization teams into Nigeria by 2010, using Geographic Information Systems (GIS) information from satellite and mobile device data to map vulnerable areas, then tracking the vaccination geo-location readings. This system provided them with the means of digitizing

Right: Aliko Dangote, Bill Gates, and Ovia.

vaccination records so that the inoculation teams could quickly and easily review which areas had been visited, and which areas had not yet had any access to the polio vaccine.

Primarily affecting children, polio is a highly infectious virus that attacks nerve cells, often causing permanent paralysis. If the viral attack is sufficiently severe, polio is fatal. While polio is entirely preventable by vaccine, once the virus is contracted by an unvaccinated individual, there is no cure. The virus has been existence since recorded human history—an Egyptian stone carving dating back more than 3,000 years depicts a man seemingly suffering from paralytic polio, and many believe that Roman Emperor Claudius suffered from the virus, causing the limp with which he was afflicted for the rest of his life.

In the early twentieth century, outbreaks of the disease became a pandemic in some industrialized countries in Europe, North America, and Australia. In the United States, the pandemic reached its apex in 1952, when some 58,000 cases were reported—of those, 3,145 were fatal, and a further 21,269 cases resulted in paralysis. The pandemic caused widespread panic amongst parents and children, in what reporters of the era sometimes referred to as "polio hysteria."

Following a breakthrough by a team of Harvard researchers studying the virus, Dr. Jonas Salk—head of the Virus-Research Lab at the University of Pittsburgh—produced a viable immunization serum. For all intents and purposes,

Salk's vaccine brought the spread of polio to a grinding halt in the affected nations, leaving stark reminders by way of canes and wheelchairs and limps of the damage it once inflicted. Celebrated survivors of paralytic polio include US President Franklin Delano Roosevelt, world-class violinist Itzhak Perlman, and Morgan Stanley Chairman Emeritus Richard B. Fisher.

As the disease was relegated to the history books in America, in parts of Asia and Africa, polio infections were rising steadily through the close of the twentieth century, and nowhere more rapidly than Nigeria, where thousands of new cases were reported each year in the 1990s. According to the National Center for Biotechnology Information, the lack of reliable, consistent, or comprehensive vaccination records was a significant factor in the poor vaccination coverage in certain regions of the country. Records were kept manually, and referenced maps that were often rudimentary, hand-drawn, or woefully inaccurate. Maps had the wrong names for some hamlets and villages, and the wrong location for others. If a village did not accurately appear on a map, it's likely it would be overlooked by vaccinators entirely. The villages would then contain pockets of children unprotected from polio, but the double-whammy is that inoculation teams could believe they had comprehensive inoculation coverage in a region that, in reality, contained these vulnerable pockets where polio could all too easily begin to spread again.

The ease of recording and analyzing reliable inocula-tion data regionally—all made possible by GIS and GPS tech-nology—proved to be a game-changer for the struggle to eradicate polio. The combined force of that technology, and the private-sector funding and drive to achieve the optimum vaccination coverage that our alliance provided proved to be an invincible force that turned back the tide of polio's contagion. At the time Bill Gates first approached us in 2010, Nigerian nationals, overwhelmingly children, accounted for more than half of all polio infections on the planet. Just three years later, the annual new-case rate was reduced to a perfect zero, and for more than two years it remained so—no recorded cases of polio at all, a feat that the Global Polio Eradication Initiative called an "historic achievement."

Coordinated with a subsequent visit to Nigeria by Bill Gates, the consortium that began with his invitation to share a vision held its official inaugural event, in March 2014. I know that I felt greatly inspired and honored as I sat on a panel alongside Aliko Dangote, Dr. Muhammad Pate, and Bill Gates—to provide a personal introduction of PHN to our audience—which included colleagues from the business, entrepreneurial, and medical worlds, and members of the print and radio/television media. The reception was overwhelming, and I believe it was clear to everyone there that the PHN was ushering in an unparalleled time in which Nigeria took its place on a global stage on which the might of big business intersects with the simple power of human kindness.

In September 2015, the World Health Organization removed Nigeria from the list of polio-endemic nations. When two new poliovirus cases were diagnosed in August 2016, the resulting disappointment was felt around the world. Circumstances existed that made the setback understandable—both afflicted patients were from the same region—a northern state that had been among the most difficult of all Nigerian states for vaccinators to reach. No one—not our own alliance, nor the World Health Organization, nor the Nigerian Health Ministry, nor Nigerians themselves—had any intention of reacting with complacency, or tolerating this small inroad the once-pandemic virus had made in our country.

Science magazine's August 15, 2016 issue ran a story about the new cases titled "Polio reappears in Nigeria, triggering massive response"—with the ensuing account that gave every impression of no resource being left untapped. The article cited the government's launch of a "massive vaccination campaign" and reported that neighboring countries were also implementing a large-scale inoculation effort to squash any possible spread from the north of the country beyond its borders. A heartening element that arose out of this setback was our growing faith in one another, crossing the public and private sectors, crossing industries and states, villages and cities—we *could* eradicate polio if we worked together. And Ebola. And malaria. We'd had a glimpse of eradication ourselves in the last several years, and with that insider's view of what could be accomplished, we moved forward, maintaining, funding, and growing this world-class private-sector powerhouse.

When NHP reached a $24.2 million private-sector donation commitment, Bill Gates matched it dollar for dollar, paving the way for the forward momentum of the Saving One Million Lives program, and when that goal is reached, we will move onto the next, and the next, powered by innovation, partnership, advocacy, and the desire to improve our world.

A LANDMARK PARTNERSHIP—
PRUDENTIAL UK

*Alliances and partnerships produce stability when they
reflect realities and interests.*
—STEPHEN KINZER, AMERICAN AUTHOR AND JOURNALIST

The course of the future can always be read by those who keep an eye on the water, watching for the telltale ripples and eddies that signify the changing of a current or the coming of a new tide. Perhaps because of my ability to intuit new opportunities in business, and to sense the next trend of supply or demand, has always come naturally to me. Most recently, that inner compass led me to give considerably more of my attention to the insurance industry, specifically its place and future in Nigeria.

Zenith Insurance Group has been offering level-term and whole-life insurance and general insurance products since 2001, with the company enjoying an annual growth rate of 22 percent of its gross written premium—the total direct and assumed premium revenue written by an insurer (exclusive of reinsurance and commission deductions). All very well and good, but an engaged investor might wonder what qualified that particular year as the optimum window of time through which to galvanize the concept of insurance in Nigeria. As ever, there is a complicated blend at work, made up of directional trends, subtle cultural evolution that accompanies a growing confidence in the market, and the serendipity that puts two top-tier players in the same space of inclination-to-growth at the same time. Opportunity, as they say, knocks—so you open the door. It is an oversimplification—but not a large one—to say it is not so much a function of the *time* being right for partnership as it is a function of the right partner appearing at a time that isn't *wrong*.

Beyond that, there must be a growth indicator, however modest, that suggests the demand for a product will be commensurate with the creation of the new supply. The basic underpinning of the insurance concept is the reapportionment of risk, moving the onus of liquidity access necessitated by accident or crisis from a single individual or business to a network, effectively transforming a single blow to a single point and spreading it out over a framework designed to absorb the impact.

In a 2017 analysis for Capital Markets in Africa, financial analyst Ada Ufomadu estimated that only 1 percent of the Nigerian population has insurance coverage of any kind. That said, there is a demonstrable relationship between economic stability and insurance penetration, measured in terms of the percentage of the total GDP to which the industry premiums contribute. As the Nigerian economy expands, companies accommodate that expansion by taking on larger levels of risk, which in turn necessitates the acquisition of insurance to weather the occasional storm of lost liquidity and stay afloat until the climate calms. For individuals, too, a growing economy brings more jobs and higher rates of pay, resulting in an increased ability to save money, and a willingness on the part of the individual to adapt his or her perception of personal finance management to accommodate a new appreciation of the benefits of risk reallocation that an insurance policy provides.

In 2015, I travelled to Cape Town to speak on a program panel at the World Economic Forum. When the program ended, Matt Lilley, the CEO of Prudential Africa, waited for me at the door, asking if I might be able to join him for coffee. My gut let me know I should oblige him. Over coffee, I learned more about Matt. Prudential Africa is a subsidiary of Prudential UK PLC, a global life insurance and financial services company.

Matt was straightforward and to the point; he wanted to do business. Specifically, he wanted to create a partnership between Prudential and Zenith Life. Nigeria has one of the youngest populations percentage-wise of any nation in the world, and while we have a strong economy we also have an extremely low insurance penetration, making us substantially underinsured as a nation. Obviously, this means that the opportunities and potential for life insurance in Nigeria are immense.

Prudential had been looking very carefully at the players, Matt told me, because they could not consider such a venture with anything but a solid and substantial company who had the right fit with Prudential, offering complementary strengths and assets that would create a mutually beneficial partnership. Given Zenith's long-standing reputation and performance as one of Africa's leading financial institutions, Prudential felt we were the ideal company in which to invest. I nodded thoughtfully, and gave him an equally forthright response. Would Zenith Life be inclined to a partnership proposal? Of course! If the price was right, and that entailed little more than our receiving a good offer. Prudential PLC was a best-in-class enterprise with a stellar reputation, in addition to being one of the oldest and most substantially capitalized insurance companies in the industry. Those first-class qualifications alone could not make a partnership—the terms had to be good. Matt understood, and assured me that he would begin putting the details of an offer together as soon as he returned to his London office. He was as good as his word—one week later, that offer was on my desk. It was, in fact, a good offer. Just not good enough.

Matt had not kept me waiting for the offer, so I did him the same courtesy, letting him know straightaway that I simply couldn't come to the table without significantly improved terms. The ball of negotiation was in his court, and again he wasted no time in sending it back into mine. I was more than pleased with his return. I saw the improvements I had been looking for, and in addition, he had presented a binding offer, meaning the key terms were essentially guaranteed, and he was formally committing to proceed. By July 2017, the deal was consummated.

Jim Ovia with Matt Lilley, CEO Prudential Africa.

The corporate genesis of this partnership is Prudential Zenith Life, a landmark transaction set to redefine the life insurance industry in Nigeria. This new transitional inroad into the insurance sector is anticipated to create thousands of employment opportunities in Nigeria, from executive and management positions to IT support staff, clerical, and sales forces—leveraging the preeminence of Zenith's local presence with one of the oldest and most successful multinational life insurance and financial services companies in operation. The Prudential–Zenith partnership creates a bancassurance agreement that creates a mutually profitable arrangement in which Zenith's banking client base and Prudential's insurance client base are afforded mutual accessibility, resulting in significant customer-base expansion.

GLOBAL SUMMITS 2017: BUSINESS AND CLIMATE CHANGE

Partnerships were far more successful than governments acting alone, than businesses acting alone, than philanthropists acting alone. The synergies of diversity were powerful in other people's lives.
—BILL CLINTON, 2017 BLOOMBERG GLOBAL BUSINESS FORUM

I travelled to New York in September 2017 as one of 250 global business executives and heads of state invited to participate in the first international Bloomberg Global Business Forum (Bloomberg GBF). The brainchild of Michael Bloomberg and the Bloomberg Philanthropies Group, the conference was designed in the wake of the financial, political, and geophysical tremors that have shaken the world in recent decades. The conference was scheduled to coincide with the United Nations General Assembly meeting for heads of state. Occasionally, a meeting of a UN Global Compact Group will occur for private-sector organizations. When that happens, people like me and other global CEOs and entrepreneurs are invited to attend, and that particular year I was also invited. During those times, there is no other city in the world in which one can find so many heads of state and high-level businesspeople. By coordinating the Bloomberg GBF schedule to coincide with the General Assembly, a significantly greater number of high-level individuals are able to attend.

Bloomberg Philanthropies describes the central mission of the Bloomberg GBF as addressing some crucial core questions, such as "... how do business leaders chart a clear path forward? How can leaders from business and government create a more transparent, equitable, and sustainable framework for the global economy? And crucially, how can political leaders, working closely with global CEOs and other business leaders, construct a new multilateral economic order to solve challenges that led to the unraveling of so many twentieth-century assumptions and institutions?" The time arguably has never been better for the serious consideration of these questions. As invited speaker French President Emmanuel Macron put it, "We are in a very specific moment. We have a lot of global challenges: climate change, migrations, terrorism—and for that, we do need multilateralism."

It was a great honor to be included in this event and to meet with Michael Bloomberg and his team, but more importantly—given my privilege to be counted amongst these global leaders—I felt I had a responsibility to attend.

With Nigeria's emergence as a growing world economy, and through the perspective of over three decades of my personal experience in multinational business and banking, I've personally witnessed that which we all know theoretically to be true—the governance and business planning of a single nation can affect the fortunes of all nations.

It is difficult to adequately convey the scope of the Bloomberg GBF attendees. In addition to President Macron of France, heads of state in attendance included Canadian Prime Minister Justin Trudeau, Ghana's President Nana Akufo-Addo, First Vice-President of the European Commission Frans Timmermans, President Ali Bongo Ondimba of Gabon, Prime Minister Mark Rutte of the Netherlands, Turkey's President Recep Tayyip Erdogan, and former US President Bill Clinton. Business leaders in attendance included Apple's Tim Cook, Jack Ma of Alibaba, Unilever's Paul Polman, Econet's Strive Masiwiya, PepsiCo's Indra Nooyi, and Bill Gates. Put simply, the invitees comprised a significant segment of the global firmament of immense resources. Esteemed company indeed, and as Michael Bloomberg joked in his opening remarks, the sum of the total net worth of those of us in the conference room would create the fourth-largest economy in the world.

Though the core-topic of the forum was globalism and globalization, one subject that came up repeatedly in panel discussions was that of climate change. At the time of the forum, the Americas were reeling from the effects of several hurricanes and earthquakes—all of historic proportions— hurricanes that flooded Texas, caused a mass-evacuation in Florida, and all but destroyed the island of Puerto Rico. In addition, two earthquakes had devastated Mexico City. Sir Richard Branson, founder of the Virgin Group, sheltered himself in a fortified wine cellar on his private island in the Caribbean during Hurricane Irma, and when he emerged he described the surrounding area as "completely and utterly devastated." In the wake of these record-making storms and earthquakes, the question of what business and world leaders can and must do to mitigate the effects of climate change was on everyone's mind.

Ovia with Richard Branson.

In the panel "Global Leaders on the Economics of Climate Change," Gabon's President Ali Bongo Ondimba was asked to describe the effects of climate change in Africa. His reply was that Africa had been battling climate change for a very long time, citing the biogeographical history of the Sahara Desert. The continent of Africa is both the geographic origin of the early human species and the location in which a large part of human evolution occurred. The Sahara extends through almost all the northern African nations from the west to east, sprawling over 3,320,000 square miles, roughly the size of the entire United States of America, making it the largest hot desert in the world. As late as 6,000 years ago, the area now comprising the desert consisted of rainforest and fertile grassland. Scientists believe a change in Earth's orbit or axial tilt may have been the cause of the change in weather patterns that saw the Sahara transform from rainforest ecosystem to hot desert, prompting the migration of inhabitants to more arable regions.

Africans, as a result, have no time to waste on those who still maintain that climate change isn't real. In this same panel, Strive Masiwiya was asked about his advocacy of an African green revolution and climate-change dissenters, to which he replied, "You cannot solve a problem that you cannot accept." Masiwiya recounted traveling to Mali in connection with the Alliance for a Green Revolution in Africa. In meeting and talking to smallholder farmers, people who by and large were poorly educated, Masiwiya found himself being corrected when he used the word "drought." It was not a drought, the farmers told him—the climate had *changed*. The help they needed was seeds that could resist the effects of that climate change. These farmers did not need to read the newspaper or attend science conferences to understand what was happening. They lived it—hence it was perfectly clear to them that the weather patterns had been altered, and as such, thinking and planning must be changed to accommodate the new reality.

It is not difficult to anticipate the chain reaction of events that climate change could initiate, especially in Africa. If it affects agriculture, it will affect food supply, and without adequate political and private-sector support, it will result in the migration of those in the afflicted areas. When you read something like this in the newspaper, it is the cause for pessimism. The unique opportunity at the Bloomberg GBF was to hear directly from those in the know—with current windows into what individual nations and businesses can do to mitigate climate change at a time when there is more public- and private-sector cooperation and more available business capital than any time before. As Engie CEO Isabelle Kocher suggested, while climate change is "a threat—it is also a fantastic lever" in the sense that it is "the very first real global challenge ... and the first time any decision made by anyone anywhere has impact on everybody." It is this unprecedented solidarity, she explained, that will enable us to tackle not just climate change, but other game-changing challenges such as poverty and food supply. Additionally, she stated that "I think our role as leaders is to look at it as a lever for action. As a group … we have decided to take our responsibilities … to fully focus our resources on what is needed to master this dual challenge—which is the battle against climate change but also to provoke development by bringing energy which as at the very core of development."

During breaks between panels, all of us had the opportunity to chat with one another, both at official receptions and in group or privately arranged dinners and breakfasts. For me, there were many old friends and familiar faces, people with whom I'm familiar with, such as Strive Masiwiya, someone with whom I'd founded charitable organizations such as Aliko Dangote, and political leaders, including presidents and prime ministers. Of course, by the very fact of their attendance, I knew that every one of us in attendance was open to or already facilitating change. For those of us who had corporations or business ventures, the very invitation is owing to not just our desire to come together to help, but also the fact that our capital resources are sufficient to allow us some latitude in the way that we make decisions, allowing for, as the moderator put it, "incorporating thoughtfulness into business planning."

As the conference exemplifies, the globalization of business has made our planet more interconnected than it has ever been before. It gives voice to many nations and continents in the framework of a great partnership made by sharing a planet. It also helps to put singular topics into focus in the context of the greater whole. I was very interested, for example, to hear Bill Gates talking—in a technology panel—about Africa's energy gap. The energy issue is at the forefront of climate-change challenges, which is why Gates established and helped to create a $1 billion fund to invest in clean-energy innovation.

Perhaps more than anything else, the Bloomberg GBF conference provided proof positive that there are certain core concepts of business that are equally applicable to any politician, organization, nation, or individual in thriving and overcoming problems from the mundane to the globally proportioned. I'll boil the concepts down to three points:

1. Avoid short-termism in decisions, operations, and policies. Achieving political power or sector-dominance while ignoring the health and needs of the surrounding community or sector is a Pyrrhic victory—akin to a harvest in the shadow of an active volcano.

2. True strength is derived from the willingness to examine your weaknesses and future vulnerabilities.

3. The greatest value of failure is its tendency to galvanize change and opportunity.

In his remarks to the audience, former president Bill Clinton observed that the longevity and resilience of the human species is attributable not to aspects of individual spirit or fortitude, but rather as a direct result of the human propensity toward cooperation. So, while it is true that the fittest survive, it is the coordination of human effort and a willingness to work as a group and share in the benefits therefrom that is the real hallmark of strength and survivorship. Across business and societal boundaries, cooperation and unification are common, but it is those undertaken with the authentic intention to benefit all participants that have the best chances for success. In big business, for example, a corporate raid may be an acquisition that is intended to provide the maximum benefit to a minimum number of individuals (such as the shareholders), and as such, it's a flash in the pan—it does not create a lasting institution, rather it dismantles the foundation of such an institution and parcels it off for maximum gain.

ZENITH TODAY, ZENITH TOMORROW: WHAT LIES AHEAD

I fundamentally believe that if you are not learning new things, you stop doing great and useful things.
—SATYA NADELLA, CEO MICROSOFT

Individuals whose businesses are personal investments of their own prosperity and security in the world can walk away from those businesses after a big merger, a record-setting deal, or when they reach an age at which it is acceptable to hang up one's hat and pursue a life of leisure. I will never be that person.

I want a strong Zenith, and I want it to move from good to great, because I believe it is of benefit to Nigeria and Nigerians. I want Zenith to continue expanding, creating new jobs, making inroads in new sectors, and continuing the crucial partnerships with the public sector to take on some of the daunting problem-solving missions on which the future of Nigeria and of the global population depends. For this reason, I will take both my business and my philanthropic ventures into the future with more momentum and promise than ever before.

My focus is the same today as it was at the start: the Zenith Bank brand. I'm cognizant of the fact that Zenith Bank is a once-in-a-lifetime branding entity—the kind of commercial mother lode that an entrepreneur is statistically unlikely to hit many times. Zenith has grown from a start-up bank among a plethora of startups to become the largest bank in Nigeria by way of its total assets to date of over $16 billion. For me, business ambition is inextricably linked with the goal of contributing to the growth of Nigeria's economy and empowering her people, which means going beyond even the creation of more than 20,000 jobs in Zenith Bank. Zenith Bank has become a great institution that is built to last—a place where people will work and grow while building their careers and achieving their dreams. Knowing that the great institution of Zenith contributes to the well-being of so many people is a tremendous source of pride and happiness.

Zenith Bank's London Stock Exchange $850 Million GDR listing, March 2013. Some attendees included, from left to right: Elaine Delaney, Quantum Capital; Omar Hafeez, Citibank; Godwin Emefiele, Zenith Bank CEO (2013), Central Bank Governor (June 2014-present); Clifford Chance's representative, Udom Emmanuel, Zenith Bank, CFO (2013); Chuka Eseka, Vetiva Capita, CEO.

We have and will continue to help local companies establish themselves and grow, businesses that may in turn employ thousands. Zenith is one of the major bankers for Dangote cement manufacturing, for example, and they now have a total of fourteen manufacturing plants both in Nigeria and internationally. Local partnerships help to keep most of the financial investment in Nigeria, essentially putting fuel into the economy, helping create confidence in the market, and, of course, contributing millions of naira in taxes, all of which play a part in the blossoming of Nigeria's economy that qualifies it as a global player. In this way I believe we have been a source of pride, having brought Nigerians the kinds of first-class services expected in modern banking—akin to what someone in London or New York would experience, including internet and mobile-banking services.

Ahmed Al Aulaqi, Vice President Banking DIFC Authority; Jim Ovia;
Arif Amiri, CEO DIFC Authority during the official opening
of Zenith Bank UK (Dubai Branch) on 31st January, 2016.

199

It is understandable for successful business enterprises to wish to move beyond their national borders and show a presence in other countries. Zenith Bank—once a Nigerian start-up—will retain its home office in Nigeria now that it has matured to a London Stock Exchange-listed global brand. Having risen to this level of success, I have every expectation that the future of our company will be bright.

In conclusion, what lies ahead for me is the pleasure and privilege of seeing the fruits of the seeds planted by the Jim Ovia Foundation. In particular, I look forward to seeing the progress of the students enrolled at James Hope College, where some of the most brilliant and gifted young boys and girls from some of the poorest homes in Nigeria enjoy full scholarship of tuition and boarding fees—seeing how these children graduate, and how each takes on the challenges of life. None of us remain on this earth forever, and I believe that we must spare no effort in ensuring that whatever we build in our lifetimes will be a springboard for the next generation as they step into leadership and assume the stewardship of our nation.

This book is intended to demonstrate that the future can hold almost anything that a well-educated and hardworking African can desire. Beyond those two qualities, I believe the driving points that will create success for any individual are available to anyone. I will summarize them here:

Right: Jim Ovia and directors of Zenith Bank at the 26th Annual General Meeting in 2017.

1. **BE VERY FOCUSED ON AND COMMITTED TO WHAT YOU DO— CULTIVATE YOUR PASSION.** If your motivation comes solely from financial profit, and not the heart, you cannot engage the passion that will take your business from good to great.

2. **HAVE FAITH IN YOURSELF, AND IN THE ENVIRONMENT IN WHICH YOU OPERATE.** Remember that everyone around you is a potential part of your future network; build that network one person at a time.

3. **GO WITH YOUR GUT,** remember that your intuition is a powerful business tool, and always pay attention to what your instincts are telling you to do.

4. **STRATEGIZE IN BRAND-BUILDING TO KEEP ALL AVENUES OF GROWTH IN THE FUTURE OPEN.** Begin locally, but with a view toward becoming global. Include the technology of tomorrow in your strategic planning of today. Without it, no business will survive and thrive in the future.

5. **BE PATIENT, AND ALWAYS DISPLAY A POSITIVE ATTITUDE.** Timing is key in all commercial enterprises. Demonstrate your own good character while strategizing to be ready for opportunity when it knocks.

6. **TURN ADVERSITY TO YOUR ADVANTAGE BY MAKING IT AN ASSET—A WINDOW OF OPPORTUNITY FOR CHANGE.** Let adversity motivate you to become vested in your own

local or business community, and to invest your time, money or resources in them.

7. **KNOW YOUR CUSTOMER.** Do the right thing always, and place value on integrity and honesty in yourself, your employees, and your customers. Always carry out proper due diligence, and expect the same from those with whom you do business.

Africa is a continent of tremendous opportunities and infinite possibilities, and our greatest years are yet to come—because Africa will continue to rise and shine!

JIM OVIA FOUNDATION PROGRAMS AND RESOURCES

JIM OVIA BUSINESSES

ZENITH BANK

www.zenithbank.com

Zenith Bank PLC was established in May 1990, and commenced operations in July of the same year as a commercial bank. The bank became a public limited company on June 17, 2004 and was listed on the Nigerian Stock Exchange (NSE) on October 21, 2004, following a highly successful initial public offering (IPO). Zenith Bank PLC currently has a shareholder base of about one million and is Nigeria's biggest bank by tier-1 capital. In 2013, the bank listed $850 million worth of its shares at $6.80 each on the London Stock Exchange (LSE).

ZENITH GENERAL INSURANCE LIMITED

www.zenithinsurance.com.ng

Vision: To be the trusted and best provider of insurance and financial services.

Mission: Ensuring peace of mind and creating value to people in a world of uncertainties.

ZGIC's clientele base spans across all strata of the economy to include but not limited to the following;

- Construction & Engineering
- Manufacturing
- Conglomerate
- Trading
- Public Sector
- Telecommunications
- Schools
- Oil & Gas
- Shipping
- Government Parastatals
- Financial Institutions
- Individuals

PRUDENTIAL ZENITH LIFE INSURANCE LIMITED

www.prudentialzenith.com

In July of 2017, Prudential PLC, one of the oldest and most strongly capitalized life insurance companies in the world, acquired a majority stake in Zenith Life of Nigeria and formed exclusive bancassurance partnerships with Zenith Bank in Nigeria and Ghana. Prudential PLC, and its affiliated companies, constitute one of the world's leading financial services groups, serving around 24 million insurance customers with £599 billion in assets under management (as of December 31, 2016). Prudential PLC is incorporated in England and Wales and is listed on the stock exchanges in London, Hong Kong, Singapore, and New York. Zenith Life was incorporated in 2001 and is Nigeria's fastest-growing life insurance company. At the end of 2017, it had ₦7.2 billion net assets and gross written premium of ₦3.7 billion.

QUANTUM CAPITAL PARTNERS

www.quantumcapital.com.ng

Quantum Capital Partners is a private-equity firm focused primarily on investing in or acquiring privately owned companies in the areas of consumer goods, agri-business, financial services, energy, telecommunications, resources, and manufacturing that have a significant business presence or operations in West Africa and/or the wider Sub-Saharan Africa region. Quantum believes that sustainable investments can be achieved through integrating environmental, social, and corporate-governance issues into our investment processes.

CYBERSPACE LTD

www.cyberspace.net.ng

With a mission to provide excellent value-added ICT services and cutting-edge networking solutions, Cyberspace has been able to distinguish itself as a complete network and software solution provider in the industry with its state of the art and world-class internet-protocol (IP) infrastructure. Cyberspace is reputed for being the first to build a world-class converged IP network that supports applications based on the three hierarchical models in 2002.

Cyberspace successfully deployed three earth stations (Hubs) across the country. The company is well positioned to provide connectivity with VSAT solutions, using both I-Direct and SCPC platform and the 3.5 GHz Fixed Wireless Access Solutions on cable technology (FWA License) acquired from the Nigerian Communications Commission (NCC) for metro connectivity within Lagos and Delta States.

ZENITH CAPITAL LIMITED

www.zenithcapital.com.ng

Zenith Capital Limited was established in November 2005 and is a former subsidiary of Zenith Bank PLC. Zenith Capital is one of the leading investment banking and asset management firms in Nigeria with strong capitalization and market turnover as well as a proven ability to execute large transactions. Zenith Capital's principal activities cover the full range of investment banking services, including corporate finance and advisory, project finance, capital markets, and issuing house. Zenith Capital's core business and experience is centered on blue chip companies, large and medium local corporates, private equity investors, government agencies, and high net worth clients. Zenith Capital has facilitated many landmark advisory/capital market deals and investments in Nigeria and across Africa.

ZENITH SECURITIES

www.zenithsecurities.com.ng

Zenith Securities Limited was incorporated in May 1990 in Nigeria and is a former subsidiary of Zenith Bank PLC. Zenith Securities is one of the leading stockbroking firms in Nigeria in terms of capitalization, market turnover, and ability to execute "big-ticket" transactions. The team provides stock-broking services benchmarked against the global best practice and leverages the latest technology to give our clients access to relevant market information combined with a knowledge-able research team. Zenith Securities' full range of services include stock broking services, securities trading, financial and investment advisory services, and related activities.

CIVIC CENTRE

www.theciviccentre.com

The Civic Centre is strategically located at the heart of Victoria Island. Its breathtaking lagoon scenery and its carefully designed, state-of-the-art, ultra-modern architectural structures create the perfect event centre.

Whether planning a gala celebration, an international conference with 1,000 delegates or seeking a private boardroom for smaller, more intimate high-level meetings, the Civic Centre has the adaptability, technology, and the range of facilities with international standards tailored to meet your needs.

The Civic Centre offers world-class facilities and standards of excellence, a vast parking lot, and a well-organized security system with a highly trained professional staff to serve its clients.

VERITAS REGISTRARS

www.veritasregistrars.com

Veritas Registrars Limited (formerly Zenith Registrars Limited) was incorporated in May 2004 to undertake the share registration business in the Nigerian capital market with a view to redefining the registrar business. Veritas, at the time of printing, manages 10 percent of the equities market in Nigeria.

Veritas Registrars Limited prides itself as a one-stop company that provides efficient and effective customer service to its teeming shareholders, leveraging on people and technology.

Vision: To redefine share registration business.

Mission: To earn the respect of all stakeholders by providing accurate, on-time share registration services using modern technology supported by expertise, innovation, and excellent customer service.

JIM OVIA NON-PROFIT/CHARITABLE PROGRAMS AND ORGANIZATIONS

ICT ENTREPRENEURS PROGRAM

www.jimoviafoundation.org/programmes/
jim-ovia-entrepreneurs-program

The Jim Ovia ICT Entrepreneurs Program seeks to empower budding entrepreneurs to tap into the emerging ICT market in Africa. The initiative seeks to nurture young entrepreneurs to their full potential over a period of twelve months.

A total of five to ten of the competitively innovative ideas are selected and funded with the goal of impacting fifty young entrepreneurs annually and selected applicants are trained by world-class professionals on developing mobile applications. In addition, beneficiaries are provided access to necessary training, counselling, and mentorship throughout the project cycle.

This initiative hosts a software-application business hackathon, where viable and innovative ideas are selected for funding. Selected beneficiaries are awarded up to $30,000 per idea. If you have a novel software or a fantastic mobile application that you want to get into the market, this is the program for you.

How to Apply: www.jimoviafoundation. org/user/login?destination=eform/submit/ muste-scholarship-application

JIM OVIA SCHOLARSHIP

www.jimoviafoundation.org/programmes/ jim-ovia-scholarship

The Jim Ovia Scholarship was founded and funded by Mr. Jim Ovia, beginning in 1998, to provide financial aid to outstanding Nigerian youths. The scholarship was previously known as the MUSTE scholarship. The awardees are given funding for undergraduate study for the duration of the undergraduate program. The award includes tuition and maintenance allowance. The scheme offers an average of 100 opportunities every year. The financial records show that as of December

31, 2017, Mr. Ovia has invested ₦225 million in the program on 1,500 beneficiaries.

Scholarships are awarded on the basis of personal intellectual ability, leadership capability, and a desire to use their knowledge to contribute to society throughout Nigeria by providing service to their community and applying their talent and knowledge to improve the lives of others. Over time it is expected that the Jim Ovia Scholarship beneficiaries will become leaders in helping to address challenges related to health, technology, and finance, all areas in which the foundation is deeply engaged.

Goals:
- To promote access to tertiary education
- To invest in the future leaders of Nigeria
- To provide a platform that encourages competitiveness and promotes equal opportunities in workplace
- To bridge the knowledge gap among Nigerian Youth

Eligibility and Criteria:

The scholarship is open to all undergraduate university students of Nigerian citizenship. One hundred awardees are selected each year from a pool of eligible applicants. Scholarships are awarded based on personal intellectual ability, leadership capability, and a desire to contribute to society at large to improve the lives of others.

How to Apply: www.jimoviafoundation.
org/user/login?destination=eform/submit/
muste-scholarship-application

EMPOWER YOUTH PROGRAM

www.jimoviafoundation.org/programmes/
empower-youth-program

Studies indicate that there are tremendous benefits of early intervention in education in the success outcomes of our youths in school graduation rates, labor-market outcomes, social welfare, and crime. The Read-Up program is an early intervention program aimed at promoting the tools and opportunities to empower the future of tomorrow. The objective is to assist marginalized youths between the ages of six and ten years to become familiarized with the digital age in a global environment by bridging the digital divide through ICT. Computers and technological literacy are an essential tool for education, business, and communication in today's world. Those without access ICT often lack opportunity and are therefore marginalized. With Read-Up, the digital divide is brought closer by providing training and access to these youths.

Our more advanced program is the **Code-Up** twelve-week immersive coding and app-development boot camp aimed at providing rigorous technology-based entrepreneurial development and leadership training for aspiring developers.

The aim is to identify Nigeria's most promising information-technology talents and empower them with skills and leadership training through our partner organizations to enable them to succeed. The goal will be to impart knowledge, skills, mentorship, and experiences that enables these youths to acquire and create technological jobs in this new digital age. Our twelve-week boot-camp program offers two tracks. Track 1 will target youths between the ages of eleven and eighteen who are selected from a consortium of select partnering schools while Track 2 will be selected finalists of the Jim Ovia ICT Entrepreneurs Program. Participants proceed on with ICT skills that will facilitate and position them to access the tech economy.

JAMES HOPE COLLEGE

www.jameshopecollege.edu.ng

James Hope College is located in Agbor, Delta State, Nigeria, and boasts of world-class facilities situated in an environment conducive to learning. Located in a developing city, the school offers the best of both worlds; the latest equipment for learning within and the ethnicity and culture of our heritage outside. September 2013 marked the very first set of students to be enrolled into the school with 50 percent of these pioneer students on a full scholarship funded by Youth Empowerment and ICT Foundation.

PRIVATE SECTOR HEALTH ALLIANCE OF NIGERIA

www.phn.ng

Vision: The vision of the PHN is to build an unprecedented world-class, private-sector-led coalition that focuses on accelerating Nigeria's progress in achieving health-related sustainable-development goals. The alliance has developed a country-owned private-sector platform to align with the government's universal-health-coverage priorities.

Mission: To mobilize private-sector capabilities to save at least one million lives by focusing on innovation, strategic partnership, advocacy, and impact investments. To build an unprecedented private-sector-led multi-sectoral coalition committed to a more structured public/private engagement that enables Nigeria to advance its progress in meeting its health goals.

JIM OVIA FOUNDATION LINKS & RESOURCES

Ovia Foundation website:

www.jimoviafoundation.org

Ovia Foundation inquiries:

enquiry@jimoviafoundation.org.ng

Ovia Foundation blog:

www.jimoviafoundation.org/blog

Private Sector Health Alliance inquiries:

www.phn.ng/contact-us

Private Sector Health Alliance blog:

www.phn.ng/blog

Private Sector Health Alliance media:

www.phn.ng/phn-in-the-news

PHN Talk Series:

www.phn.ng/phn-talk-series

ADDITIONAL RESOURCES

Harvard Business School Executive Education: Owner President Management Program: www.exed.hbs.edu/programs/opm/Pages/default.aspx

Mastering Negotiation Strategy: Learn to focus on "a difference that matters" in the Owner/President Management Program, video link: www.exed.hbs.edu/assets/Pages/video.aspx?videoid=3522

Bill and Melinda Gates Foundation: www.gatesfoundation.org

Bill and Melinda Gates Foundation Blog: www.impatientoptimists.org

Gatesnotes, Bill Gates' Blog: www.gatesnotes.com

Bloomberg Philanthropies: www.bloomberg.org

Bloomberg Global Business Forum: www.gbf.bloomberg.org

Bloomberg Philanthropies Blog: www.bloomberg.org/blog

Richard Branson's foundation Virgin Unite:

www.virgin.com/unite

Virgin Money Foundation:

www.virginmoneyfoundation.org.uk

Richard Branson's Blog:

www.virgin.com/richard-branson

APPENDIX A
ADDITIONAL LINKS

Central Bank of Nigeria: www.cbn.gov.ng

Nigerian Communications Commission: www.ncc.gov.ng

Federal Ministry of Finance: www.finance.gov.ng

MTN telecommunications: www.mtnonline.com

Globacom: www.gloworld.com

Airtel: www.africa.airtel.com/nigeria

9Mobile: www.9mobile.com.ng

Sprint: www.sprint.com/globalroaming

Econet: www.econetwireless.com

APPENDIX B
RECOMMENDATIONS FOR FURTHER READING

The Road Ahead by Bill Gates, Viking Press, 1995.

The Bright Continent: Breaking Rules and Making Change in Modern Africa by Dayo Olopade, Mariner Books, 2015 (revised edition).

Too Big to Fail: The Inside Story of How Wall Street and Washington Fought to Save the Financial System—and Themselves by Andrew Ross Sorkin, Penguin Books, 2010 (revised edition).

Losing My Virginity: How I Survived, Had Fun, and Made a Fortune Doing Business My Way by Richard Branson, Crown Business, 2011 (revised edition).

The Rise and Fall of Nations: Forces of Change in the Post-Crisis World by Ruchir Sharma, W. W. Norton & Company, 2017.

Climate of Hope: How Cities, Businesses, and Citizens Can Save the Planet by Michael Bloomberg and Carl Pope, St. Martin's Press, 2017.

Tap Dancing to Work: Warren Buffett on Practically Everything, 1966-2012 by Carol J Loomis, Portfolio, 2012.

Stress Test: Reflections on Financial Crises by Tim Geithner, Broadway Books, 2015.

The Innovator's Dilemma: The Revolutionary Book That Will Change the Way You Do Business by Clayton M. Christensen, HarperBusiness, 2011 (revised edition).

Competing Against Time: How Time-Based Competition is Reshaping Global Markets by George Stalk Jr. and Thomas M. Hout, Free Press, 2003.

The Intelligent Investor: The Definitive Book on Value Investing. A Book of Practical Counsel by Benjamin Graham, Jazon Zweig, and Warren E. Buffett, HarperBusiness, 2006.

Playing to Win: How Strategy Really Works by A.G Lafley and Roger L. Martin, Harvard Business Review Press, 2013.

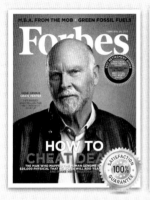